PLATO

A BEGINNER'S GUIDE

ROY JACKSON

Hodder & Stoughton
A ... E GROUP

Orders: please contact Bookpoint Ltd, 130 Milton Park, Abingdon, Oxon OX14 4SB. Telephone: (44) 01235 400400, Fax: (44) 01235 400500. Lines are open from 9.00–6.00, Monday to Saturday, with a 24-hour message answering service. Email address: orders@bookpoint.co.uk

British Library Cataloguing in Publication Data
A catalogue record for this title is available from The British Library

ISBN 0 340 80385 1

First published 2001
Impression number   10 9 8 7 6 5 4 3 2 1
Year 2007 2006 2005 2004 2003 2002 2001

Copyright © 2001 Roy Jackson

Cover photo from Corbis Images.
Typeset by Transet Limited, Coventry, England.
Printed in Great Britain for Hodder & Stoughton Educational, a division of Hodder Headline Plc, 338 Euston Road, London NW1 3BH by Cox & Wyman, Reading, Berks.

CONTENTS

Who was Plato?

As one of the founding fathers of **philosophy** and best known of the thinkers of Ancient Greece, Plato has had a massive impact on the history of Western thought. He lived from around 427–347 BC, spending most of his time in Athens.

WHY IS PLATO'S WORK SO IMPORTANT?

Plato was very creative and a great innovator. However, no one works in a vacuum and there were a number of outstanding philosophers

before him who influenced his work. As none of their writings exist, if indeed they wrote anything at all, little is known about these shadowy figures. Nonetheless, from references in other works, it is apparent that the term 'philosophy', for most of them, covered a broad and varied school of thought. What they generally all have in common is a concern with matters of **cosmology** (from the Greek word *kosmos,* meaning something like 'good order'). The ancient Greek philosophers were intent on finding a unifying principle of the cosmos, an order for the apparent chaos of the world they occupied.

Although also concerned with matters relating to cosmology, Plato and his teacher Socrates (c. 470–399 BC) are very different from the so-called 'pre-Socratic' philosophers before them because of their more rigorous and rational method of enquiry. What they did was to invent the method and terminology of philosophizing that is still used today. By introducing analysis, cogent argument and a rational approach to thought Plato especially laid the foundations for all philosophers who came after him. This is why the British philosopher Alfred North

Whitehead (1861–1947) famously said that the history of philosophy is but 'a series of footnotes to Plato.'

Rather than being pre-occupied with grand theories of the universe Plato's main concern initially was with **moral philosophy**; with how we ought to live our lives. However, although this was his main inspiration, as he matured his writings covered many of the branches of philosophy, including **political philosophy**, education, **aesthetics**, **metaphysics,** and **epistemology**. Plato was also something of a poet, and his writings are regarded as not only monumental works of philosophy, but great literature. Plato is the earliest philosopher whose writings have survived and so they provide an important insight into the culture and beliefs of the complex and cosmopolitan society of Athens as it existed two-and-a-half thousand years ago.

> **KEYWORDS**
>
> Moral philosophy, also known as ethics. The study of issues such as if there is such a thing as good or bad and how we can determine this.
>
> Political philosophy, the study of political systems and the asking of questions such as 'Why should we obey rulers?'
>
> Aesthetics, or the philosophy of art – concerned with such questions as 'What is beauty?'
>
> Metaphysics, concerned with the nature of ultimate 'reality'.
>
> Epistemology, also known as the Theory of Knowledge, and so concerned with where our knowledge comes from and whether it is 'true' or not.

Plato founded the Academy in Athens and this institution has often been described as the first European university. Here people studied works of philosophy, mathematics, politics and the sciences for nearly a thousand years. A great deal of religious thought in Europe was intermingled with Plato's philosophy, for example, in the writings of the Christian theologian St. Augustine (AD 354–430) and in medieval Islamic thought where it was translated and preserved in Arabic. Plato's works were later re-translated into Latin and Greek as it emerged as a force during the Renaissance. In the nineteenth century, Plato's work was a basis for Victorian values in Britain. His controversial political and educational views have played an important part in more recent debate. It is certainly true to say that no student of philosophy can afford to ignore Plato and his work.

PLATO'S WORLD

Plato was born around 427 BC, probably in Athens or the nearby island of Aegina. He was given the name Aristocles, but was called Plato which means 'broad' or 'flat', a possible reference to his broad shoulders (he used to wrestle). He was born into a wealthy political family. His father, Ariston, was descended from the last king of Athens, and his mother was descended from the great Athenian law-maker Solon.

To understand Plato and his philosophy it helps to have some idea of the world in which he lived. Greece at that time was not one united country, but a collection of semi-autonomous 'city-states' (in Greek, **'polis'**)

KEYWORD

Polis, a Greek word for 'city-state'.

that were united by language and culture, as well as a defence against powerful external enemies, notably Persia. During Plato's long life he witnessed the decline and fall of this Greek federation. It was an age of war and political upheaval, yet it was also a period of great cultural

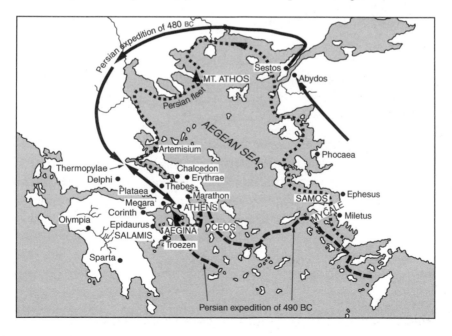

Persian expedition of 490 BC

activity. Athens, especially, was an exciting and sophisticated place. The famous Parthenon, a temple dedicated to Athena, was built in the mid-fifth century BC, and Plato would also have been able to see some of the greatest Greek tragedies performed in the squares and theatres of the city. Yet Plato's philosophy, his belief in order and suspicion of democracy, was also moulded by the political climate of the recent past:

* Between the eighth and sixth centuries BC, Athens and Sparta became the two dominant cities of Greece. Each of these city-states united their weaker neighbours into a league under their dominance. Sparta, a state Plato admired for its order and discipline, was highly militarized and ruled by force and oppression. Whereas Sparta established its league largely through conquest, Athens unified mostly through mutual and peaceful agreement.

* In the early part of the sixth century BC, a limited form of democracy replaced hereditary Athenian kingship. This was the start of the greatest period of Athenian history economically and culturally. The Athenians also succeeded in defeating an invading Persian fleet, despite seemingly overwhelming odds. As a result, Athens became the most influential state in Greece and the voluntary Delian League was formed with Athens at its head. However, as Athenian power grew it became more tyrannical towards other states in the league.

* During the fifth century BC, under the leadership of Pericles, Athens entered its golden age. The Parthenon was built during this time; a time of tragedians such as Aeschylus, Sophocles, and Euripides. The constitution was reformed to make it more democratic. During the latter half of the century, however, Athens was constantly at war with Sparta. Most likely Plato would have fought against the Spartans in the cavalry.

✳ In 405 BC Athens was defeated by Sparta and the victors established an **oligarchy** over the city known as the Thirty Tyrants. Two of these 'Tyrants' were close relatives of Plato. This reign, however, lasted for only a year or so before democracy and independence were restored, but Athens was now in decline, as was the whole of

> **KEYWORD**
>
> Oligarchy, the rule by the few, also known as a plutocracy. Rule is established depending upon how much wealth you possess.

Greece. Its northern neighbour, Macedonia, began its expansion, which would eventually lead to Macedonian supremacy under Alexander the Great from 336 BC.

SOCRATES

During his lifetime, Plato witnessed the decline of Athens and experienced the moral uncertainty that resulted. Plato was born into a wealthy and politically powerful Athenian family, and he was encouraged to enter politics himself, but his experience of unscrupulous politicians and the constant strife amongst various political groupings soon disillusioned him. However, Plato had a deep concern for the welfare of Athens and its citizens and so it was philosophy he looked to as a way of voicing these concerns. At around the age of 20, Plato encountered a remarkable man: Socrates.

Little is really known about Socrates and yet his name stands out amongst the ranks of great intellectuals. He was born in the region of 470 BC and spent his life in virtual poverty. The lack of money was of his own choosing, being more concerned with living the 'examined life' as he called it. The concerns of Socrates were mostly ethical, determining what is the best life and the best society to live in. He survived through the generosity of friends and disciples, Plato being one of them.

Plato wrote in the form of a dialogue in which various characters discuss philosophical issues, and it is through these dialogues that Socrates has become a familiar name to us. Socrates would always be the main character who would interrogate people in a form that has

become known as the **Socratic Method**, or
what Socrates himself described as the method
of the 'midwife'. Socrates always said that he
knew nothing, only the skill of hauling out
knowledge from others, and so he believed that
truth was innate and could be extracted rather
like a midwife extracts a baby from its mother.

In Plato's dialogues, Socrates engages in
conversation on topics dear to the hearts of
many Greeks: piety, courage, justice, and
beauty amongst other things. If someone said

KEYWORDS

Socratic Method, A term
used to describe Socrates'
converational technique
of using dialectic.

Dialectic, A method of
attempting to get to the
nature of truth by
questioning concepts. The
Socratic Method is a form
of dialectic.

that he or she were pious, Socrates would retort with, 'What do you
mean by piety?' and, forced to provide a definition, it would be
demonstrated that such a concept was based on weak assumptions and
uncertainties, forcing the individual to modify his or her view. It was a
process of **dialectic** by which the aim is to achieve a more accurate
definition. The intention was to show that we cannot be confident in
our knowledge and, in fact, much of what we believe has no rational or
logical basis. Further, Socrates believed that the closer we can get to the
correct definitions, then the closer we will be to the truth.

He was deliberately provocative. It was for this reason Socrates jokingly
referred to himself as a gadfly; biting away at his victims. As a result of
this he made many enemies and, in 399 BC, he was placed on trial for
'corrupting the youth' with his ideals. He was condemned to death and
refused to escape or adopt the traditional method of proposing another
form of punishment such as exile (which probably would have been
accepted). He preferred to die with dignity and remain a good citizen
of the State that he so dearly loved. In choosing his method of death he
drank a cup of hemlock and died within half an hour.

PLATO THE PHILOSOPHER

The death of Socrates had a profound impact upon Plato.
Undoubtedly, the fact that his friend and teacher was condemned by

democrats was one reason Plato distrusted democracy and, as he saw it, the rule of the mob. He was determined to keep the spirit of Socrates alive by engaging in philosophy in the Socratic tradition.

However, Plato's own safety was compromised by his close friendship with Socrates. It is, perhaps, for this reason that Plato decided to leave Athens and undertake a 12-year exploration of the known world. His travels included Egypt where he was impressed by the theocratic system, the rule by an educated priestly class. It is even speculated that Plato reached the banks of the River Ganges but, despite certain similarities between his own philosophy and eastern religions, it is an unlikely hypothesis. What is more credible, however, is his encounter, in Italy, with the **Pythagoreans**; a community founded upon the principles of Pythagoras (c. 582 – c. 500 BC). In around 530 BC, Pythagoras settled in a Greek colony in southern Italy called Crotona where he established and led a tight-knit community of like-minded people. Pythagoras's teachings survived and spread over Greece and southern Italy. These communities were well ordered and strict in terms of diet, dress and moral codes.

The Pythagoreans believed in the immortality of the soul and in **Reincarnation** as well as a belief that nature was subject to a mathematical order. The name of Pythagoras is, of course, associated with the mathematical theorem that equates the square of the sides of a right-angled triangle to the square of its hypotenuse – the nightmare of many a schoolchild! However, the theorem was most likely developed later on by his followers. Nonetheless, the importance of mathematics and the belief that 'all is number' had a profound effect on Plato. For Pythagoras, numbers held the key to understanding the universe. Everything could be explained in terms of number, which existed in an abstract and

KEYWORDS

Pythagoreans, communities that followed the teachings of Pythagoras, which included a belief in the immortality of the soul, reincarnation and the importance of mathe-matics in determining reality.

Reincarnation, the belief that, after the death of the body, the soul transfers to another body.

harmonious realm beyond the flux of the everyday world. It was the Pythagoreans who discovered the link between number and musical harmony and envisioned the movement of the planets as the 'music of the spheres'.

Plato, too, believed there is a timeless unchanging order to the universe and that there is an underlying 'form' to the world that can, through reason and mathematics, be perceived. It is said that above the door to his Academy was written, 'Let no one unacquainted with geometry enter here.' What developed was Plato's famous **Theory of the Forms**; the very 'essence' of the universe that provides the key to knowledge.

KEYWORD

Theory of the Forms, Plato's theory that the universe has an underlying order consisting of 'Forms' or 'Ideas' which could be ascertained through the power of human intellect.

Plato also travelled to Syracuse in Sicily, the most powerful city-state west of the Greek mainland. The ruler of Syracuse, Dionysius, seemed keen to discuss philosophy with Plato, but it turned out that Dionysius was an impatient and intractable individual and expelled Plato from his land after a series of arguments. However, during his time in Syracuse, Plato had a long and turbulent relationship with the ruler's brother-in-law, Dion, for whom he wrote poetry and described him as the lover who drove him mad with desire.

At the wiser age of 40 Plato returned to Athens and bought a plot of land in the Grove of Academe, named after a mythical hero called Academus. Here Plato established a school of intellectuals modelled on the Pythagorean model. When Plato was about 60, Dionysius died and was succeeded by his son, and Dion's nephew, Dionysius II. Dion persuaded the reluctant Plato to return to Syracuse to teach the new ruler to be a 'Philosopher King' in the mould of Plato's own political views. However, like his father before him, the new ruler proved a reluctant and impatient philosopher and, once again, Plato fled back to Athens, preferring to stay out of politics from then on.

Plato, who never married, died at the age of 80 and was buried in the Academy. The Academy itself continued to thrive producing such notable alumni as the philosopher Aristotle (384–22 BC) and developing important schools in, for example, mathematical science and astronomy. The Academy was closed down by the Roman Emperor Justinian in AD 529. This is roughly the time that saw the birth of the Dark Ages.

PLATO'S WORKS

Plato's works can be divided into three periods: early, middle and late.

* The early period was concerned mostly with moral issues and was heavily influenced by Socrates. Although it cannot be said for sure, it is quite possible that much of this work is really the philosophy of Socrates and does not contain much originality from Plato himself. Nonetheless, these are great literary pieces, especially the *Apology*, *The Crito, Euthyphro*, the *Laches*, the *Charmides*, the *Protagoras*, and the *Gorgias*.

* When we enter the middle period, the character of Socrates expresses a greater concern with such issues as politics and metaphysics, which demonstrates more Plato's philosophy; although still using Socrates as his mouthpiece. The middle period, then, was Plato at his peak, producing important works such as the *Meno*, the *Phaedo*, the *Symposium* and, best known of all, the *Republic*. The *Republic* is a rich book in which all aspects of philosophy are connected together in a grand scheme for the kind of state Plato wished for. A state ruled by the wisest and best: the 'Philosopher Kings'. These rulers would be the wisest because, through training in the sciences especially, they would have learnt how to gain access to truth itself: the Forms. It is not just a book on political philosophy, but provides views on education and a theory of human nature based upon his belief in the eternal soul.

＊ Plato's later works are less dramatic and original. Much of these works, such as *Parmenides*, are merely a development of Plato's earlier philosophy. However, the *Timeaus*, which may belong to the later period (although some argue it is part of the middle period), contains an interesting **creation myth** of a divine craftsman that

> **KEYWORD**
>
> Creation myth, myths that relate how the world was originally formed. Common amongst most religions, for example, Genesis in the Bible.

imposes order on a chaotic world. This echoes Plato's own concern for order and the belief that such logical and systematic structures do exist.

＊ ＊ ＊SUMMARY ＊ ＊ ＊

● Plato is famous because he is a founding father of the methods in philosophy.

● He was heavily influenced by the political and cultural climate of his time.

● Plato decided to become a philosopher through the teachings of his mentor Socrates. He was a strong proponent of the Socratic Method.

● His philosophy is a combination of the teachings of Socrates and such thinkers as Pythagoras.

● Plato is best known for his writings during the middle period, especially:

– His Theory of the Forms, which is the belief that there is an underlying order to the universe.

– His political views developed in the *Republic*, which argues that the State should be ruled by the 'wisest and best': Philosopher Kings who have knowledge of the Forms.

– His views on human nature, which include a belief in the soul and the importance of reason.

● Plato established an Academy to promote the study of philosophy and the sciences.

The Socratic Method 2

Plato was hugely influenced by his teacher Socrates, and it is not possible to appreciate Plato's teachings without first considering those of his mentor.

Socrates was born when Athens was at its peak. It was the greatest power in the Mediterranean, a major trading centre, the world's first democracy and the centre of a mighty naval empire. Its ruler of the time, Pericles, embodied all of the achievements of Athens; a self-made man and a hero who had defeated the mighty Persians. Gathering the finest sculptors and craftsmen from around the Greek world, Pericles invested in a massive reconstruction programme which included the building of the Parthenon. This remarkable temple was completed in just 15 years. In the main auditorium stood a 40-foot high statue of the goddess Athena, made of gold and ivory and studded with precious jewels. The Parthenon, which can still be visited today, became the spiritual heart of the city and a symbol of the power of Athens.

Yet at the death of Socrates, the city of Athens was ruined by war. Its people had lost everything, Pericles had died from the ravages of a plague that had killed a third of the city's population, and what was supposedly an enlightened city was responsible for the execution of its greatest mind. How could such a thing have occurred?

THE TEACHINGS OF SOCRATES

Speaking of Ancient Athens, the British philosopher Bertrand Russell (1872–1970) said, 'It was possible in that age, as in few others, to be both intelligent and happy, and happy through intelligence.' Though perhaps an over-romanticized vision, it nonetheless has an element of truth. Philosophers, scientists, physicians, mathematicians, astronomers, artists, architects, all flocked to Athens to network and discuss their theories with their peers. If the Hellenic League was the United Nations of its day, Athens was its New York.

Athens, during its golden age, was enjoying a time of relative peace and prosperity, when many Athenians, bathed in self-confidence, were garbed in expensive robes and enjoyed luxurious food and wine. However, there was one man who would wander the streets of the Athenian marketplace, known as the Agora, in his bare feet and dressed in unkempt and dirty garments. This man, Socrates, was considered the ugliest man in the city, for his head was too big, his nose misshapen, and his eyes bulged. In every sense, he seemed the very opposite of the fine classical lines of Grecian beauty. In itself this tells us much, for his followers were not concerned with superficial looks, but what lay behind: the beauty of his mind.

Plato's early dialogues deal with subjects that were of interest to Socrates. Although it is difficult to know where Socrates' philosophy ends and Plato's begins we can, with a certain degree of certainty, place Socrates' thought under three main categories:

* **Rejection of traditional beliefs**. Socrates was always prepared to throw out coveted traditions and beliefs if he thought them to be wrong, and he encouraged his followers to do likewise.

* **Concern for ethical issues**. Socrates was concerned mostly with morality and the belief that there can be universal definitions for such terms as 'goodness'.

* **Conversation as a practical method in acquiring knowledge**. People learnt from Socrates through conversation. Conversation was a means, a logical process, by which definitions are attained and truths acquired.

REJECTION OF TRADITIONAL BELIEFS
Socrates was certainly not unique in questioning the beliefs of his time. What was different was the *way* he questioned them. Socrates would

have encountered some of the greatest minds of his time, as well as being able to explore the beliefs of their predecessors. It was a period when the enlightened Greeks, with time on their hands, could wonder about the origins of the universe and our place within it. As a result, many began to question the traditional beliefs in the gods and goddesses, and the creation myths contained within such works as Homer's *Odyssey* and *Iliad*. In many respects, this was the beginning of science as we understand it today: the attempt to look for material, rather than spiritual, explanations for the universe.

Socrates's Conversion

As a youth, Socrates was attracted to the beliefs of the **physicalists**, or **materialists**, who tried to understand the universe in purely material terms, rather than appealing to the gods. For example, Demosthenes argued that nature can be reduced to the basic building blocks, which he called atoms. However, Socrates soon rejected this form of 'natural philosophy' as being unable to provide useful knowledge.

KEYWORD

Physicalist/materialist, a person who believes that the world is made up of nothing but matter and that it is possible, therefore, to reduce all things to the basic fundamentals of matter.

Instead, he turned to the nature of man and his relation to society.

In Plato's work, the *Apology*, it is recorded that Socrates experienced a 'conversion'. Socrates' friend, Chaerephon, had visited the famous Delphic Oracle to ask its priestess whether there was anyone wiser than Socrates. The priestess replied that there was none wiser. Socrates took this to mean that the truly wise man is one who recognizes that he is really ignorant. Socrates adopted this as his own philosophy based on the pronouncement of the Delphic Oracle, 'Know thyself'. Socrates was a great believer in the power of human reason to learn absolute truths. To discover the truth is to *know* what it means to live the good life and to live it virtuously.

In one of Plato's works, the *Meno*, the character of Meno asks Socrates the following question: 'Can you tell me, Socrates, whether goodness is a thing that is taught; or is it neither taught nor learnt in practice, but comes to men by nature, or in some other way?' In this one question we have the very essence of what was both Plato's and Socrates's concern: what is the right way to live? For 'goodness' can be variously translated as 'virtue', 'excellence' and so on, and is from the Greek **arete**. So, what does it mean to be good, and how can we know this 'good' and teach this to our children? This is as much a concern today as it was in Plato's time; and we can see how it encompasses not only moral philosophy but also politics, education and the question as to where our knowledge comes from.

CONCERN FOR ETHICAL ISSUES

The Sophists

Whereas Socrates believed in absolute standards, there was a group of itinerant teachers, the **Sophists**, who thought the opposite. The greatest Sophist of all, Protagoras, famously declared that 'Man is the measure of all things.' By that he meant that it was mankind that established what is right or wrong, not the gods or the existence of a morality independent of man. Again, we can see parallels with the world we live in today: with the decline in institutional religion and the increase in the view that there is no one truth. This raises the question of how we can teach moral standards when there are no 'standards', only what is relative. This is what is meant by **moral relativism**, and it was this especially that both Socrates and Plato found abhorrent.

KEYWORDS

Arête, a Greek word which can be translated as 'excellence' or 'quality'. Plato believed that all things have an 'arête'. For example, the arete of a pair of scissors is to cut. Humans, too, have an arête. The difficulty is in determining what this is.

Sophist, a Sophist was, amongst other things, a relativist. Sophists were teachers who believed that there is no such thing as true knowledge. What is 'true' is what society believes or is persuaded to believe.

Moral relativism, belief that morality has no universal and absolute standards, but is relative to a time, place or person.

To understand what goodness meant for the ancient Greeks it helps to look at how the children were educated at that time. In the golden age of Athens, the sons of the aristocrats – for they were the only ones who received any kind of decent education – were brought up to imitate the virtues of the gods and heroes contained in the works of, for example, Homer and Hesiod. 'Virtue', for most ancient Greeks, did not mean the same thing then as it does for the Western European of today. For the Greeks, virtue included such attributes as courage, ambition, the acquisition of wealth, glory and acting for the good of the *polis*.

The Sophists, however, were more concerned with teaching people to be 'clever' rather than the training of character. For example, today both Hitler and Napoleon might be considered 'clever' politicians, yet neither would be considered virtuous in our modern sense of the term. However, we might be more prepared to see Napoleon as having more character and nobility than Hitler. Many of the great Athenian heroes were leaders who would certainly not pass the test of being good by our modern standards; Pericles being a typical example of this. However, Pericles was also seen as possessing the qualities admired and praised in the Greek myths, such as courage and nobility and a genuine concern for the interests of the State. However, for the Sophist, what mattered was the acquisition of *power*, not the kind of person you were.

For the Sophists, the laws of one society are no truer than any other. Morality was a matter of the conventions of the society you lived in. Later Sophists were more concerned with a desire to make money and win arguments by whatever means. Socrates considered them to be nothing more than illusionists who could make people clever speakers but without possessing virtue or selflessness. During Socrates' later years, the politicians in power practised more and more the arts of sophistry, reflecting the general decline in moral standards in Athens at that time.

CONVERSATION AS A PRACTICAL METHOD IN ACQUIRING KNOWLEDGE.

The Socratic Method

The dialogue style of writing is particularly associated with Plato's work because it is so unlike the writing of previous philosophers, which usually took the form of a long treatise using technical language and the impersonal third-person. The leading character in his dialogues is usually Socrates and so they are often referred to as Socratic dialogues. Characters are created within a scene and engage in spontaneous conversation; not unlike a playwright would present his work. It is not surprising that Plato's works are also considered great pieces of literature. Why did Plato adopt this form? In a way it was a tribute to his mentor, for Socrates always believed that knowledge came through conversation. Remember, he himself never wrote anything down, preferring the cut and thrust of lively discourse. For Plato to recreate the character of Socrates it made sense to present his words as a dialogue. By using this form, Plato himself is acknowledging the soundness of the Socratic method; the use of dialectic to get to the truth.

In terms of how the dialogue is structured, Plato commonly uses the following approach, which is an example taken from *Euthyphro*:

* **Socrates begins with a simple question in which nothing is presumed**. For example, in the *Euthryphro*, Socrates, in his usual modest fashion, asks to be the 'pupil' of the much younger and somewhat naïve Euthyphro. Socrates begins by asking: 'Then tell me, how do you define piety and impiety?'

* **The question is then examined and definitions given**. Euthyphro would go on to define what piety and impiety are: 'What is agreeable to the gods is pious, and what is disagreeable to them impious.'

* **Assumptions are questioned**. Here Socrates would then leap in and raise the further question as to whether we can assume that what the

gods do are always right and also that the gods themselves seem to contradict themselves.

* **Conventional views are dismissed or redefined**. Euthyphro, for example, is then compelled to alter his original definition: 'I should say that piety is what all the gods love, and the opposite, what all the gods hate, is impiety.'

Now Socrates, having forced Euthyphro to redefine what he meant by impiety, could well sit back and leave things at that but, like the gadfly that he is, he pushes on. Reading the dialogue you can sense Euthyphro's growing unease and frustration as he is compelled to redefine yet again until, eventually, the redefined view of piety bears no resemblance to its original description. In the meantime, the conversation will have meandered along through all kinds of objections that could be either relevant or irrelevant to the original topic.

Like the characters in a novel, each has his role to play. The characters were often taken from real life, but Plato would embellish them to bring out sharp contrasts; making them more bullish, arrogant, complacent, impatient, careless, assertive, aggressive, etc. than they actually were. This was necessary for dramatic effect, although it can result in making Socrates seem rather unreal at times, just too good to be believable. But every story must have its hero.

Socrates believed in the importance of conversation as a method to determine the truth of things. Through a careful process, involving defining terms, questioning those definitions, and then moving to a further definition, Socrates believed we could eventually reach a clear and unalterable definition for such things as 'goodness'. This ties in with his belief that there actually can be one true understanding of goodness, unlike the Sophists who argued that goodness is merely a relative term depending on the time and place.

It could be argued that being taught the skill of persuasion, of getting on in life, of 'how to win friends and influence people' can, indeed, be a very useful skill to possess. This was true enough and the reason Socrates was usually associated with the Sophists is because he himself used the same techniques. However, an important difference is that Socrates said that his aim was to determine the truth of things, whereas many of the Sophists were not concerned with truth, or even believed that there was such a thing as truth: only persuasion. It was this ability to persuade that worried Plato and Socrates: a Sophist could claim to *persuade* a sick man that he could heal him better than any doctor, even though the Sophist lacks the medical skills required.

Being clever could be used for both good and bad purposes. You might consider a modern parallel with the spin doctors in politics today whose primary purpose is to manipulate the perception of politicians and their policies so as to make them palatable to the public. A clever Sophist could persuade the sick man to be healed by him, but this does not make him a good doctor either in the moral or technical sense. For both Socrates and Plato, the concern was to produce good people. Therefore, a good ruler should be someone who was both virtuous and technically skilled to rule in the same way a doctor is both morally concerned to make his patients well and technically skilled to do so.

For Socrates, as well as Plato, it was important to educate people in the truth. Inevitably this raises the question of what *is* truth. Right at the beginning of the *Meno*, Socrates says he does not know whether goodness can be taught without first determining what goodness *is*. This is a sensible enough remark to make: you should understand what something is before you set out to teach it. Therefore, if we are to teach what is right to our young we must know for sure what *is* right. Here, to know something is to be aware of the truth of something, and so differs from what we may call 'opinion'.

THE SCAPEGOAT

During Socrates's latter years, the city of Athens was in decline. Its defeat by Sparta in 405 BC had been a massive blow to its confidence. The trouncing and subsequent ravaging of the land led the people of

Athens to question what had gone wrong. Why had such a mighty power fallen? In seeking a scapegoat, the masses – led on, no doubt, by the politicians themselves who followed the prejudices and passions of the masses to gain support – blamed Socrates. Athens, seeking security, returned to its old traditions and saw in Socrates a man who most publicly questioned the belief in gods and the old ways, as well as corrupting the youth with his ideas.

When Socrates was arrested he could, like the Sophists, have gained the sympathy of the public if he had wished, but he remained stubborn and resolute to the end. He neither sought sympathy nor forgiveness, for he believed he had done nothing wrong except to seek out the truth. After his death, Socrates, in time, did become a new kind of Greek hero replacing the more militaristic figures such as Pericles. Socrates represented the person of conviction who follows the dictates of intellectual conscience and it was this legacy that Plato promulgated.

* * * SUMMARY * * *

● Plato was hugely influenced by his teacher Socrates.

● Socrates taught that a philosopher should question traditional beliefs.

● Socrates had a great concern for ethical issues, on what is the right way to live. He was critical of the materialists who believed you could reduce all knowledge to the building blocks of nature.

● Socrates believed that it is possible to have absolute standards. In this he was the opposite of the Sophists who were moral relativists.

● He also believed that conversation is the best method for acquiring knowledge. This developed into the Socratic Method.

3 The Forms

The death of Socrates had a profound impact upon Plato. Any political ambitions he had were now of no concern to him. He was disillusioned with politics and saw his mission to carry on the legacy of his mentor, to be a philosopher. After a number of years travelling and soul-searching, Plato returned to his native Athens and began to teach and write. His early dialogues were records of conversations that Socrates might have had with various individuals. For example, with Euthyphro on what it meant to be pious, or with Crito on the subject of civil disobedience.

Plato also wrote an *Apology*, which was a defence of Socrates against his critics. However, it was one thing to defend the life of Socrates, it was another to demonstrate that the 'examined life' was the best life to live. To achieve this Plato set out to prove that philosophy, more than any other profession, was the noblest profession. In this sense Plato was going much further than Socrates, for his mentor never claimed to know anything; to have absolute knowledge of truth. It was this belief that we can have true knowledge that developed into Plato's famous **Theory of the Forms.**

THE ANALOGY OF THE CAVE

One reason why Plato has remained so popular after all these years is that he was aware of his audience. His dialogues were designed for popular consumption, and there is evidence that Plato did not write down his more advanced philosophy, as it was not meant for the general public. He appreciated the importance of explaining often difficult concepts in a way that could be more readily understood. To achieve this, Plato often made use of **analogy**. An analogy is when you make a relationship between two or more entities to bring out their similarity; for example, to make an analogy (though not a very good one) between the structure of an atom and the solar system. To explain his Theory of the Forms, Plato used the now well-known Analogy of the Cave.

KEYWORD

Analogy, using an analogy is a way of explaining an often difficult concept by showing its similarity to more familiar things.

This analogy is from Plato's most famous book, the *Republic*. As usual in his dialogues, the main character is Socrates. It is Socrates who describes the cave to his fellow conversers:

* Deep down at the very bottom of the cave is a group of prisoners. The prisoners are firmly shackled so that they cannot move, or even turn their heads. They all face only one direction, the wall of the cave. These prisoners have been in this condition since they were young children.

* Behind the prisoners a fire burns away, and between this fire and the prisoners there are many people who are walking by, talking and carrying artificial objects such as figures of men and animals made of wood and stone. The people walking by are hidden by a screen, so that only the artificial objects appear above the top of the screen.

* The fire casts a shadow of these artificial objects upon the wall of the cave. It is this wall that the prisoners can see. The prisoners are not aware of what is happening behind them and so, for them, the whole of their reality consists of shadows on the wall. They can only see shadows of the artificial objects and so, in a way, are seeing shadows of shadows. When they hear talking or other sounds they believe it comes from the shadows.

* One day, one of these prisoners is let loose from his chains and is forced to turn around, look and walk towards the fire. The released prisoner finds all of these actions painful and is dazzled by the light,

having spent his life in almost complete darkness and not being able to move. He is told that the objects he now sees are the real objects and that what he had experienced all his life were mere shadows.

* Confused and frightened, the prisoner wants to return to the bottom of the cave, but he is dragged further away and up towards the entrance. Faced by the daylight he is unable to see a single object. Only gradually, over time, can he grow used to it, first by perceiving the lights of the night sky, then the shadows of objects cast by the sun and finally the objects themselves in broad daylight.

* Eventually, after a period of getting used to the light of day, the released prisoner is even able to gaze at the sun itself.

A more modern analogy today would be the cinema, where the audience would watch the play of shadows thrown by the film coming from a light behind them. The audience would believe that the events in the film are real to them as opposed to the events outside the cinema.

The Path to Enlightenment

As Socrates tells his tale he asks his colleagues to imagine what the prisoner must have thought and felt during this whole experience. The released prisoner's initial reaction is fear and confusion; a desire to return to the comfort and security of what he had lived with all his life, *even though* he has been told that it is an illusion. Forced to experience the world outside, he undergoes a gradual awakening; an awareness that there is a more beautiful and real world so very different from the dark world of shadows where he has spent all his life. In time, the prisoner also realizes that all things he had cherished and felt were so important to him previously now no longer matter. The chained prisoners would, amongst themselves, gain status and honour by attempting to determine the sequence of events that would occur amongst the shadows. The released prisoner, however, realizes that this quest for glory was illusory.

By perceiving the sun itself, the prisoner becomes aware that it is the source of all things; it produces the changing of the seasons and controls everything in the visible world, including the fire and, from that, the shadows that he used to think were the only reality. Aware of all this, the prisoner would rather be 'a serf in the house of some landless man' than to be the person he was before he was released.

Socrates then speculates on what would happen if the prisoner was to return to the bottom of the cave; not to return to the life he led but to tell the other prisoners what wonderful things lay beyond the darkness of their experience. He asks us to imagine how the others would respond to this. Would they welcome him with open arms and want to see this world for themselves? Quite the opposite, Socrates thought. For the released prisoner, having grown accustomed to the outside world, would fumble in the darkness and could no longer engage in the complexities of divining the motion of the shadows. The prisoners would see him as a fool, a bumbling idiot. In fact, if he made any attempt to free them from their shackles, they would gang together and kill him.

With this in mind, even if the prisoner knew that his colleagues at the bottom of the cave would not understand him and that his own life would be in danger, Socrates thought that the prisoner should return. To keep his knowledge to himself and allow his colleagues to remain in ignorance is a crime.

This curious tale works on many different levels. What is it meant to teach us? First of all, his audience will have known who the prisoner represents: it is Socrates himself. The man who had no concern for the conventions of everyday society, of the quest for glory or honour. The man who talked of higher things, who saw it as his mission in life to tell people that their dearly held beliefs were a sham. The man who was often mocked because of his appearance and lack of practical sense. Ultimately, the man who many feared and whose life was not only in danger but, in the end, was ended by those who refused to understand. In a much broader sense, the prisoner is every philosopher: the searcher for truth – whose purpose in life is to teach this truth to others.

THE REALM OF THE FORMS

The Analogy of the Cave is not only about the quest of the philosopher, however. It is also a way of explaining Plato's Theory of the Forms. What are the Forms? In the story *The Little Prince* by the French poet and writer Antoine de Saint-Exupéry, the author recounts how, as a young boy, he lived in a house where there was supposed to be some buried treasure. The treasure was never found, but the possibility that it might exist gave the house a special quality and beauty. As Saint-Exupéry says, 'What is essential is invisible to the eye.' Apparently, the sculptor Michelangelo, when receiving praise for his work, would retort that all he had done was to remove the excess marble in the block and so reveal what was already there. In a sense the Forms are what is 'already there', but we usually cannot see them and instead are concerned with the excess marble.

In the *Republic*, the character of Socrates points out that his analogy is a picture of the human condition. People are trapped by the illusory world of the senses; they are like the prisoners at the bottom of the cave. However, Plato believed that the ability to perceive the truth behind this illusion is contained within our very souls. The Forms are the world beyond the shadows. We take the shadows to be reality, but is really only appearance. It is no coincidence that this Realm of the Forms bears some resemblance to the Christian concept of heaven, as Plato's philosophy had considerable influence on the development of Christian thought.

For Plato, this is not the real world. The real world is invisible. It lies beyond our senses of sight, taste, touch, smell and hearing. So what led Plato to believe that there is such a world beyond this one?

The Form of Beauty

We can see many beautiful things; a beautiful flower, a beautiful painting, a beautiful woman, and so on. But what is *beauty itself?* In other words, how do we know that so many different objects all share the attribute of beauty? One response to this might well be that we learn through experience. However, Plato believed that our knowledge of beauty is *innate* – we are not born an 'empty slate' with no knowledge at all, but possess within our soul all knowledge already. The trick is to be guided towards that knowledge.

Other Forms

In fact, it is not just beauty, but *everything* appears to have a Form. For example, an object such as a table has a Form of a table. Although tables differ from each other in size, colour, texture and so on, they all share the attribute 'table'. Likewise, if we talk of a letter-box being red, a car being red, an apple being red, then they all partake in the Form 'red'.

Try to draw a circle. How does it look? Depending upon how steady your hand is your circle will most likely be imperfect in some way or other; it might be a little pear-shaped. But how do we *know* what a perfect circle is? How do we know that every time we attempt to draw a circle it isn't 'quite right'? For Plato, it is because there is a Form of a circle, and this tells us something about what the Forms are. They are perfection. When you see a beautiful flower it is not perfectly beautiful, but *partakes* in perfection. Similarly a table could be functional but you might well be able to conceive of a better table; one that is sturdier and longer-lasting.

If you can perceive that one piece of furniture is better than another, Plato raises the question how do we *know* it is better? What is this 'better' that we are aware of? We can see how this affects many aspects of life. When we say that society, quality of life, morality, etc. is progressing then we are making the assumption that there is something to progress towards. Plato, as well as Socrates, believed that there is such a thing as moral truth; that morality is not a relative matter; dependent upon the society or time you live in. When one society claims to be more morally advanced than another it is the same as saying there is such a thing as independent moral standards.

If we return to the Analogy of the Cave, our prisoner's journey towards daylight is an educational one. Through proper training – that is in becoming a true philosopher – he will attain knowledge of the Forms and, as a philosopher, it is his *duty* to return to the cave and enlighten his fellow man. At the same time, the Forms cannot be taught. We know them already but refuse to acknowledge them, for to do so would be a painful and confusing process; it takes us away from the security of our illusions. The prisoners in the cave are, for Plato, the people of Athens. They are in a state of ignorance. Even the highest amongst them – the politicians and educators of Plato's Athens – have no greater knowledge than the 'lowest'.

The Form of the Good

In the Analogy of the Cave, the Form of the Good is represented by the sun. The sun is the source of all things; it gives light so you can perceive other objects, and it gives life to all things. The sun is responsible for the changing of the seasons, for the weather, for the food, we eat.

Plato believed that there is a hierarchy of Forms. Whereas there are particular Forms for beauty, for justice, for a chair, a bed and so on, there is one Form over and above all of these; the Form of the Good. All existence and perfection ultimately flows from the Form of the Good. Like the sun, it gives light and life to all other things, including the other Forms. Therefore, when you have awareness of the Form of the Good you have achieved true enlightenment. When the early Church Fathers developed Christian theology, they borrowed heavily from the works of Plato. In Christianity, the Form of the Good becomes God: the source of all things, immutable, eternal, perfect and invisible.

The following provides an outline of what these Forms are:

* The Forms represent Truth or Reality. This cannot be attained by the senses (touch, taste, smell, sight, hearing) rather by the exercise of the mind. That is, through the use of the intellect. The word 'Form' is the conventional translation, although in Greek the term 'eidos' or 'ideā' would translate better as 'idea'. However, this perhaps suggests that the Forms, or Ideas, are contained within the mind, whereas Plato is adamant that they are independent of the mind.

* The world of sense-experience (the objects we see, touch, taste, feel and smell) partake in the Forms in that they contain likenesses of, for example, perfect beauty, good, red, and so on. When we recognize that an object partakes in, for example, the Form of Beauty, it is because we recollect our knowledge of the Form of Beauty that was acquired before birth. In other words, our knowledge of the Forms is innate, we are born with it and, through a process of education, we are able to *recollect* this knowledge.

* The Forms are eternal and unchanging, whereas the world of the senses is temporal and changing. In that sense we cannot know things that are in a constant state of flux, for what is there to know?

CRITICISMS OF THE FORMS

The Theory of the Forms has perhaps caused more controversy and confusion than any other aspect of Plato's philosophy. Here is a brief outline of just a few of the concerns raised by the Theory:

* Is there a Form for literally *everything*? For example, if you can reduce the world to the most basic particles, is there a Form for atoms, or even a Form for the nucleus of an atom? In which case, is anything really universal and static?

* Connected with the above concern, to what extent can you reduce the Forms to objects? Is there a Form for the planet Earth? Can there then be separate Forms for all the objects of the earth?

* In what sense do these Forms exist? Plato talks about the Forms as distinct and separate 'things' that are immutable, perfect, eternal and invisible, but what does this really reveal about their actual nature?

* In terms of there being Forms for morality, how is it possible to separate morals from everyday actions? The philosopher Aristotle, Plato's one-time pupil, believed morality couldn't be eternal and unchanging. Can there really be ultimate moral standards?

* Plato also argued that if a person *knows* what is right and wrong, he will *do* what is right and avoid what is wrong. For example, if you have knowledge of the Form of Justice and, from this, you know it is wrong to steal, then you will not steal. Is this a realistic view of human nature?

In his later works, notably the *Parmenides*, Plato seems more open to the difficulties and criticism of his Theory of the Forms. Nonetheless, Plato's belief that there exists a Realm of the Forms is prevalent throughout the philosophy of his middle period especially, and so we will encounter it, and some of the concerns expressed above about it, when we consider his views on not only epistemology, but human psychology, education, politics, ethics and religion. Despite the obvious problems with the Theory, the main point is an important one: if there are such things as absolute standards then where do they come from?

* * *SUMMARY* * *

• Plato used the Analogy of the Cave to demonstrate his Theory of the Forms.

• Abstract concepts such as beauty and justice have a Form, as well as concrete things such as chairs and beds.

• The Forms are eternal, perfect, invisible and unchangeable. They are the archetypes of the things of sense perception.

• The Form of the Good is the ultimate Form and gives light and life to all other Forms.

4 Knowledge, Opinion and Ignorance

To better understand what Plato meant by the Forms it helps to consider his views on knowledge. For Plato we can only have knowledge *of* something. This might sound obvious enough, but you can see how this would be affected by his Theory of the Forms, for if what we see around us is not real, then it follows that what we think we know is not really true knowledge. If that is the case, then how can we have knowledge of anything at all, and where does this knowledge come from? For Plato, the obvious answer is the Forms, but we need to examine how he came to this conclusion.

PROTAGORAS AND RELATIVISM

In one of Plato's dialogues, *The Theaetetus*, the question of what is knowledge is discussed. This is Plato's epistemology. Theaetetus is a young mathematician who, when engaging in conversation with Socrates, is asked what knowledge is. Theaetetus replies, 'In my opinion anyone who knows something perceives that which he knows, and so, as it seems at the moment, knowledge is nothing other than perception.'

Here Theaetetus is presenting the common view most famously presented by the Sophist Protagoras: 'Man is the measure of all things.' You know something when you perceive it; that is, taste, touch, hear, smell or see it. However, Socrates is quick to point out that our sense perceptions can be a very subjective matter:

＊ For example, someone who comes in from the cold will put his hand in a bucket of cold water and it will feel warm to him. Or when you drink some sweet wine when you are ill it tastes bitter. How can the same object have a different quality? Which understanding of the object is the *correct* one?

✳ Why should it only be 'man' who is the measure of all things? If a human being's perceptions are real for him, it would logically follow that a pig, a baboon or even a tadpole's perceptions are also real for it! This is actually a very insightful point and is a concern that has been raised by more recent philosophers. The German philosopher Immanuel Kant (1724–1804) thought it somewhat arrogant of man to think that what he perceived is actually *there*. Rather, we can see things only through 'human spectacles'. We see things in three dimensions (four dimensions if you want to include time as the fourth), but who is to say that there are not higher dimensions?

✳ Perhaps most importantly, if we are to say that each human being is to be the judge of what is and what isn't, then it is not possible to make judgements of the views of others. If one person was to say that an apple is green and another that it is red then there can be no definitive judgement one way or the other. On a more personal level, Socrates was having a go at Protagoras, who happened to be a teacher. Surely, if there are no absolute standards, a teacher cannot teach what is right and wrong?

Theaetetus's response to Socrates latter criticism is by talking of perceptions as being *useful*, rather than true or not. As a modern day example, we might not be able to say whether the traffic light shows red or green, but it is worthwhile for the teacher to correct someone who claims the light is green when everyone else sees it as red. This may seem an unsatisfactory answer, for in this case knowledge seems to be based on nothing more than what the majority may perceive.

It comes down to what the purpose of the teacher is: to promote harmony, order and social standards in the same way the doctor's role is to promote good health, *not* that good health is an objective thing that we must therefore pursue. However, Plato rightly points out that what is useful or worthwhile can hardly be synonymous with what is morally right. If a state decides it is 'useful' to condemn innocent people to death this does not make it right. Ultimately, Plato's concern is that we should not confuse knowledge with perception, or that all knowledge simply comes down to a person's opinion.

DO YOU REALISE, SIR, THAT YOU JUST PASSED A RED LIGHT

AND WHO'S TO SAY IT DIDN'T PASS ME?

HERACLITUS AND CHANGE

Plato, as well as Socrates, was familiar with the writings of the philosopher Heraclitus, although Socrates had once said of Heraclitus' book *On Nature*, that, 'The part I understand is excellent, and so, I dare say, is the part I do not understand; but it needs a Delian diver to get to the bottom of it.' Heraclitus, who lived around 500 BC, was known for his philosophy of 'Becoming' – his most famous phrase being, 'You cannot step into the same river twice.' Although you may still give the river the same name, its continuous flow has meant that the water has moved, and the life within it has moved and changed. For Heraclitus, the world is in a constant state of change and flux. All objects are *becoming* something else, they are not constant. For example, the chair you may be sitting on is ageing and wearing down, even rocks are being eroded by the wind and rain. Human beings, too, are changing all the time. Every seven years, each molecule of your physical body has changed. You are no longer the same physical person! When you look at a photograph of yourself as a baby, the only thing that has remained the same is your name.

AND HERE'S A PICTURE OF MY ATOMS WHEN I WAS FOURTEEN

Heraclitus viewed the world as a vast battlefield of conflicting, opposing forces, all governed by a natural law that controls this strife between the elements. This natural law he called **Logos**, which can be variously translated as 'word', 'truth', 'reality', 'reason' or

KEYWORD

Logos, Greek noun which can be variously translated as 'word', 'truth', 'reality', 'reason' or 'God'.

'God'. However, for Heraclitus, this was not some metaphysical substance, but is contained within nature itself and is more akin to DNA than God.

This view of the world, however, was anathema to Plato. Plato adopted a view not dissimilar to an earlier Greek philosopher, Parmenides (c. 500 BC), who believed that the *Logos* is One, and is therefore immutable. If the world is in a state of constant change, then there can be nothing that is eternal and immutable and, of course, there can be no ultimate truths. Plato believed that, although the world might *appear* in a state of change and multiplicity, it is possible to perceive an underlying form and singularity.

Plato's main criticism of Heraclitus is that, if it is the case that things are constantly in motion, then it is impossible to define a thing. For example, 'white' cannot be called white if it is actually becoming something else (not white). How then are we able to call something white? In fact, if you wish to call something black then it is just as correct as calling it white; neither one of you can be wrong or right. Every answer, on whatever subject, is correct. This would also be a criticism of Protagoras for, if all of our knowledge comes from perception, then all of our knowledge must be correct, no matter what it is.

For Plato, therefore, it was unacceptable that our understanding of the world, of our views on good or bad and so on, are merely relative (Theaetetus) or continually changing (Heraclitus).

THE PHILOSOPHER DEFINED

In *The Republic*, Plato provides a definition of the philosopher. The philosopher is someone who loves wisdom. In fact, this is the very translation of the phrase '*philo-sophos*': 'wisdom-lovers'. Socrates makes it clear that these must be distinguished from '*philo-theamones*': 'sight-lovers'. Sight-lovers are those who go from one play, book, exhibition etc. to another, taking it all in and calling this knowledge. You might consider the modern analogy of the snap-happy tourist, taking pictures of great monuments without really appreciating what he sees. The philosopher, therefore, is not superficially acquiring facts and figures, but is reflecting on the very nature of things.

Importantly, Plato wishes to make a distinction between when you say you know something, and when you say you believe something. If I say that I *know* that the earth is round, this is different from saying I *believe* that the earth is round. Following on from Parmenides, Plato held that

you can only have knowledge of *what is*. If I *know* that the ε
round, then it really *is* round. However, opinion (or belief) can b   r
what is *and* what is not. If I say that I believe the earth is round (what
is), it *could* really be flat (what is not).

Plato was concerned that people seem to have completely opposite
views on the same thing. For example, someone might judge a painting
as beautiful, whereas someone else would judge it as ugly. Another
example is with morality; someone might consider a certain act as just,
whereas someone else would consider it unjust. In this sense, it is belief,
not knowledge. You are part of the multiplicity of things, of things that
are and are not (the painting both is beautiful and isn't beautiful). The
philosopher, however, is concerned only with what is eternal and
immutable.

It also follows that if you perceive what is not, then you are in a state of
ignorance. You may have a belief that something is not beautiful when
in actual fact it is.

Objects of knowledge	= the Forms	= what is
Objects of opinion	= the 'many things' that partake in the Forms	= what is and is not
Objects of ignorance	= nothing	= what is not

THE ROOTS OF KNOWLEDGE

For Plato, things that can be qualified do not count as knowledge. For
example, Helen of Troy is beautiful, but not *unqualifiedly* beautiful (she
may be ugly when old; therefore 'is and is not' beautiful), or giving back
what you owe is not *unqualifiedly* just (for example, giving back a
weapon to a madman). **What is knowledge is what cannot be
qualified. They are not subject to time, place or the perspective of the
individual**. This is why Plato, through Socrates, would also get his
interlopers to qualify their statements in the hope that, eventually, a
definition could be reached in which it could no longer be qualified.

Only then have you achieved what *is*. The French philosopher Rene Descartes (1596–1650) believed that if we are to discover what we can know for sure we must begin by sceptically doubting our supposed knowledge of all things. We must reject our beliefs in a wholesale manner and start all over again. Plato, however, does believe that our beliefs can help our understanding, not hinder them. We must look to our beliefs first, rather than be sceptical about them.

THE ROLE OF REASON

How are we to attain this knowledge of the Forms? Plato was a **rationalist**. He believed that you cannot rely upon the senses for your knowledge and that, ultimately, the power of reason is the key to knowledge. Many more recent philosophers, known as **empiricists**, argue that all of our knowledge comes from experience of the world. That is, we only know that, for example, two plus two equals four because we have *experienced* the adding up of these objects. Plato, however, believed that this knowledge is something we can know merely by using our reason, without reference to the outside world.

> **KEYWORDS**
>
> **Rationalist**, rationalism is the belief that we can use the power of reason alone to acquire knowledge.
>
> **Empiricist**, empiricism is the belief that all our knowledge comes from our senses, from our experience of the world.

For Plato, therefore, reason plays a crucial role in the acquisition of knowledge and is an essential part of his political and educational agenda. When Plato spoke of the Forms residing in the soul of each man, he also perceived the soul as the seat of the *intellect*.

✳ ✳ ✳ *SUMMARY* ✳ ✳ ✳

● Plato rejected the belief that 'Man is the measure of all things' because then you are forced into relativism. There can be no truths.

● Plato also rejected the belief that the world is in a state of flux because it would then not be possible to know anything.

● As it is possible to have knowledge it is the duty of the philosopher to seek out this knowledge.

● Our beliefs are important in that they provide a foundation for knowledge. They are a starting point.

5 The Soul

Plato, along with his one-time student Aristotle, had a massive impact on Christian theology. For Plato, this is perhaps most prevalent in his **dualism**; the existence of two independent worlds – the Realm of the Forms and the world of the senses – and the existence of two independent parts of the human being – the immaterial soul and the physical body.

KEYWORDS

Dualism, a belief that there are two separate entities.

Psyche, a Greek term that can be translated as 'soul' or 'life principle'.

Neither the Old nor New Testament contain a belief in such a dualism; a separation between the material body and an immaterial soul. The Creeds explicitly state a belief in the resurrection of the *body* (although St. Paul considers this a 'spiritual body'). In the early centuries of the Church, Christian theology employed the ideas of Plato into its doctrine, and only then did the idea of an immaterial soul come about.

The Greek work *'psyche'* suffers somewhat in translation, and perhaps 'soul' is not the best definition because of the specifically religious connotations that have come down to us. A better translation might be something like 'life-principle'. However, as 'soul' is the common usage, it will be used here.

Our main source for Plato's views on the soul can be found in his work the *Phaedo*. In this work, Socrates is in conversation with some friends in his prison shortly before his execution. On such an occasion, it is not surprising that Socrates speculates upon the nature of life after death, and the belief in an eternal soul. As with all of Plato's works, we need to be careful as to how much these views can be accredited to Socrates, especially as Plato himself was not actually present on this occasion.

PREPARING FOR DEATH

In the *Phaedo*, the character of Socrates explains that the true philosopher should look forward to death and that they should ready themselves for dying. Like the whole of Plato's philosophy, his views on life after death are interlinked with his belief in the eternal Realm of the Forms. As this world is transient and unreal, the philosopher should surely wish to escape the distractions of the body and the world around him so that he can dwell in this realm of pure thought.

The body is seen, then, as a hindrance, a distraction; the desire for food, sensuous satisfaction, illness and so on are all weaknesses that get in the way of the mental pursuit for truth. The philosopher, in order to attain knowledge of the Forms, is in a constant battle with the world of the senses, and must engage continually in a process of what Plato described as *katharsis*.

Katharsis

The Greek word '*katharsis*' has come down to us as the English '**catharsis**', which usually means to relieve an emotional or neurotic condition by relating, usually through drama, a traumatic experience that has been repressed. It is used even more commonly when people talk of reading a book, seeing a film, or listening to music that they find to be 'cathartic', that is, it allows them to let go of suppressed feelings and emotions.

> **KEYWORD**
>
> Catharsis, to relieve emotional or neurotic condition by means of relating a traumatic experience that has been suppressed.

Katharsis, for Plato, was also a form of purification. Plato was deeply influenced by the mystic group known as the Pythagoreans, who practised a form of regular purification of the body by using types of herbal medicines, fasting, and the practice of music, dance and song.

It is certainly not uncommon today, even in the secular world, for people to feel the need for an occasional purification, even if it is simply taking a day out from eating now and then. Amongst most religious traditions, forms of purification – most especially through lengthy periods of fasting – are common practice, and are a means of getting more in touch with the spiritual side of one's being, rather than being pre-occupied with the bodily needs. More extreme forms of self-purification can involve a degree of self-mutilation, for example in cases of flagellation as a form of religious discipline and penance.

Plato believes that the philosopher, by means of various austere practices, can be aware of the delusion of material gain and sensuous pleasures and instead be close to the Truth, which, in effect, is close to death. In death, the soul is released from the body and so is no longer subject to its distractions. In such a case, Plato argues, why should the philosopher fear death?

THE NATURE OF THE SOUL
The soul, Plato believes, is eternal. At the death of the body the soul continues in a disembodied existence as *pure intellect*. Plato makes clear links between the concept of the soul and the intellect here. The soul is actually possessed of intelligence as it resides within the Realm of the Forms. Therefore, when the soul enters the body, so does intelligence. Education is not acquiring new knowledge, but *recollecting* what the soul possesses already. To attain knowledge you need to look within your own soul.

Reincarnation
Plato also believed that the soul, once freed from the body, is weighed down by the corruption of the sensual world. If the person who dies has lived an immoral life, then the soul will be reborn into a vice-ridden existence. Drunkards and greedy people are reborn as asses, while tyrants will be reborn as birds of prey. However, if you have lived a virtuous life you may be reborn as a better human being. This idea would have seemed curiously foreign to many Greeks, and resembles more the Hindu concept of reincarnation.

The three parts of the soul

In another of Plato's dialogues, the *Phaedrus*, Socrates is talking to a young man called Phaedrus while sitting under a tree in the countryside. Socrates is talking on the nature of the soul. The soul is immortal, with no beginning and no end. Further, it is immortal because the *ever-moving is immortal*. This description of the soul as 'ever-moving', as something that is also moved by its own accord, and not by something else, is a property that is not mentioned in the *Phaedo*. However, remembering that the soul is perhaps best translated as 'life-principle' it would make more sense for the Greek mind to conceive of the soul, the *psyche*, as containing movement as one of its properties, for all life is in motion.

In a famous image, Socrates presents a simile to describe the soul's nature:

* Imagine the soul to be a chariot with a charioteer and two winged horses; one white and one black.

* The charioteer and the two horses together represent the three parts of the soul.

* The charioteer represents the rational part of the soul.

* The white horse represents spirit and energy.

* The black horse represents the appetites.

Leaving aside whether to believe that there is an actual soul or not, Plato does present an interesting view of psychology; as a struggle between the various elements of the psyche. As an example of how these three parts might interrelate, imagine you have a craving for a cigarette. This is your appetite, the black horse, talking, and it would be a simple matter to give in to the craving and have a cigarette. Yet your reason, your charioteer, tells you that it is bad for your health, one cigarette will lead to another, and so on. Reason alone, however, is insufficient to stop you from having the cigarette, what is also needed is courage and spirit, the white horse, to prevent you from doing so. Hence, if reason, along with spirit, work together and rule over the appetites you will not have that cigarette!

PLATONIC LOVE

The significance of *winged* horses is that it is the natural tendency of the soul to strive upwards, towards the Realm of the Forms. In his later dialogue, the *Symposium*, the soul is not only controlled by the intellect, but is

KEYWORD

Eros, the god of love in Greek mythology.

driven by desire, by the god of love, **Eros**, to unite with the eternal realm. However, the soul is trapped, imprisoned within the physical body. The black horse, of course, strives to move downward, while the white horse strives to fly upward. When the soul becomes entrapped within a body, its wings are destroyed. Socrates describes how true love helps these wings to grow once more, and therefore to be released. It is the natural state of the soul to gaze upon the forms of justice and beauty. When we gaze upon a beautiful object we are, therefore, 'recollecting' the pre-existence of our souls within the Realm of the Forms. The soul, therefore, is also the seat of love.

Plato's Eros is the soul's impulse towards the Form of the Good. At the lowest level, this manifests itself in our desires for a beautiful person and our wish for immortality by having children with that person. At a higher level, love involves a spiritual union which leads to good within a social sense. However, the highest kind of love is the love of wisdom, of philosophy which, ultimately, can lead to the vision of the Form of the Good itself.

What is interesting here is the move away from the emphasis on reason and intellect for the soul's escape to the later work that emphasizes love as a way for the soul to grow and escape the world of the senses. In his middle period, Plato believed that the appetites were dangerous and needed to be controlled by reason, whereas in later life he gives the sensuous pleasures freer reign. However, Plato is keen to point out that the highest form of love, platonic love, is to get away from pure sensual pleasure and to ascend to the blissful vision of beauty itself. Plato argued that the power of beauty is its ability to cause us to recollect the Realm of the Forms from which our soul has descended into the body. This particular interpretation was developed especially by the mystical elements of religious traditions with the emphasis on a love and union with God.

THE COSMIC SOUL

In the *Republic*, Socrates makes reference to the 'maker of the heavens', and it is unclear what he means by this. What is the relationship between the Realm of the Forms, the gods, and the world of the senses? Is there a Creator God and did this God also create the Forms?

In Plato's later work, the *Timeaus*, Plato describes the whole universe as a living entity that has both body and soul. The Cosmic Soul rules the universe, including the gods such as Zeus. However, this Cosmic Soul was itself created by the 'Demiurge', a Divine Craftsman that created the whole universe using the eternal Forms as its model.

This Demiurge exists, therefore, separately from the Forms, but is also separate from the Cosmic Soul. The Demiurge, rather, created the universe in its own image, but it is lesser than the Demiurge because, like human beings, it is contained within a body. Therefore, the Forms act as the perfect model for the Demiurge to create the universe. Whereas the Forms are perfect, eternal and unchangeable, the universe, as it is made of matter, is imperfect, temporal and changeable.

As an example, imagine a sculptor who wishes to create a statue of a beautiful person but, as he is limited by his materials, creates something that can give the *appearance* of the beautiful person, but inevitably is a poorer image of the original. Nonetheless, it is possible to look within the sculpture and see the beauty within it. Here you perceive the true Form of the beautiful person, rather than its image, its 'shadow'.

Christian doctrine, of course, could not accept the belief in Forms that were separate from God, because then God would not be the creator of everything. Rather the Forms become ideas within the mind of God, who then creates the universe from these ideas.

✹ ✹ ✹ SUMMARY ✹ ✹ ✹

- Plato was a dualist. He believed that the body and soul are separate entities and that the soul is eternal.

- Through purification ('katharsis') it is possible to be closer to the soul and, therefore, to the eternal Realm of the Forms.

- The soul is the seat of the intellect. At the death of the body, the soul resides in the Realm of the Forms. It is then reincarnated into another body.

- The soul has three parts that battle with each other for supremacy. If you allow the soul to be ruled by the appetites then you lose touch with the soul and are concerned only with bodily pleasures.

- The soul's natural craving is to be in the Realm of the Forms. Plato's later philosophy talked of the desire for beautiful things as a way into the vision of the Form of the Good.

- Plato developed a whole creation myth involving a Cosmic Soul that was created by a Demiurge and which existed separately from the Realm of the Forms. The Forms act as the Demiurge's perfect model for the creation of the universe.

How Are We To Live? 6

Plato's Theory of the Forms and his views on the concept of the soul have important implications for his political and educational philosophy. His work, the *Republic*, represents Plato at his peak and it is important as it incorporates all of his views in a comprehensive system. It is very easy to isolate one aspect of his political philosophy without appreciating how it connects to his views on epistemology, morality and so on. This would be a mistake, and it has caused many critics to declare Plato as totalitarian, anti-liberal and elitist. To an extent these criticisms are justifiable, but should be tempered by considering the age Plato lived in as well as his genuine concern for the welfare of his beloved state and the importance he placed on the practicality of his political theory *only if* it is actually possible to access the Realm of the Forms. This by no means excuses him, but it should help to understand him.

What is so special about the *Republic*? What sets it apart from other philosophical works? The *Republic* is one of the world's greatest works of philosophy and literature. It is Plato's magnum opus and it set the standards and boundaries for future Western philosophy. It is the first major work of political philosophy and presents a comprehensive and radical theory of the State that views the role of the State as not merely an agent of control, but as an agent of *virtue*. The State is an educational tool to nurture, nourish and develop individual behaviour. In this respect, Plato had great faith in the ability of the State to wield its power wisely. However, the *Republic* is more than just a political theory, for it is also very personal. **The individual is an indelible part of the State, the two cannot be separated**.

JUSTICE

In presenting his political agenda, Plato is also concerned with the personal lives of individuals. At the very beginning of the *Republic*, the character of Socrates asks, 'What is justice?' But the word justice is a somewhat unsatisfactory translation of the Greek word **dikaisunē**. The word covers both personal and social morality, and so the concern is with the right way to live both for the individual and the community. By asking what is justice, Socrates wants to address the broader question of duties and obligations, of the individual's role in society. These are profound and important questions that are as relevant today as they were in Plato's time. Why should I be good? What do I owe the State, and what does the State owe me? What is the meaning of right conduct? In the *Republic*, the political and personal are merged, for the individual mind is ultimately shaped through the political system. Plato is only too aware of how powerful the environment is in moulding character.

> **KEYWORD**
>
> *Dikaisunē*, a Greek word which is often translated as 'justice'. However, it has a much wider meaning. It concerns the central issue of what is the right way to live your life and how you know that you are leading a good life.

Polemarchus and the conventional view of justice

In the *Republic*, Plato, through the character of Socrates, begins by asking Polemarchus what justice is. Polemarchus, being a man shaped by the traditions and conventions of his time, looks for an answer by referring to the traditional texts and the revered poets of his day. He quotes the poet Simonides who says that you should give every man what is due. This is essentially the 'eye for an eye' view of justice: if someone does good to you, then you should return this; if someone does you bad, then you should do bad to him. This is how Socrates responds to this view:

* Socrates wonders whether it is ever right to harm others. Long before Gandhi stated that an eye for an eye and the world would go blind, Plato questioned whether a morality could really be based

upon harming others. Of course, it may be *expedient* to do so, but this does not make it morally *right*.

✳ *Socrates talks of each person possessing what is called arête, which can be translated as 'excellence' or 'quality'.* He points out that if you harm a horse you make it less excellent than it was before and this could be applied to people. Harming people does not make them better people, but worse.

✳ Socrates then presents an important analogy. He compares the ruler to that of a physician. It is an analogy Plato makes throughout the *Republic.* The physician takes the Hippocratic Oath: *do no harm.* What if this oath was applied to rulers?

✳ For a state to be a moral state it is important to elicit the moral qualities in each individual. Here, Plato is also presenting his educational agenda: you cannot force people to be good, to be excellent (*arête*); you must teach in a way that brings out the individual's distinctive qualities. Teaching is a *process*, not something that is inflicted upon the individual. It is essentially through the Socratic Method that this is achieved.

✳ Therefore, can it be right conduct (i.e. justice) to detract from the individual's special excellence (*arête*)? The state, in its role of educator would have nothing to gain and much to lose if it were to force or intimidate its people into being good.

Thrasymachus and the unconventional view of justice

Having silenced Polemarchus, the important character of Thrasymachus presents his radical and unconventional view of justice. Thrasymachus was a real historical character, a Sophist and a skilled teacher. He believed that there are no eternal truths and that our beliefs and values are relative to the time and place we live in. As a relativist, he denies tradition. In this way, Thrasymachus can be seen as the antithesis of Polemarchus.

Thrasymachus's new premise is this: **might is right**. There is no eternal standard of justice, only a standard of power. It is the rulers who define justice, for they have the most power. In fact, Thrasymachus goes even further than this by presenting another, related premise: **The person who is unjust is the happier person**. Thrasymachus presents an image of the 'superman'; a powerful figure who is self-assertive, establishes his own values and defies conventional morality. Consequently the unjust are not only happier, they are more successful.

This cynical view of justice is a powerful one, but it is important for Plato to refute it for the implications would be a society which has no absolute standards of morality and is concerned only with the pursuit of power and happiness. How does Plato's character Socrates respond?

* Socrates re-introduces his analogy of the ruler and the physician. The physician's primary concern is with the interests of the patient, not only his own. Granted, the physician exercises his power over the patient's body, the power of knowledge, but he does not use this selfishly, for personal gain. Remember, he must follow the Hippocratic Oath: do no harm.

* Why, Socrates argues, shouldn't politics be just as professional as medicine? Medicine has knowledge, it is a science. Physicians practise their science for the common interest. Why cannot there be a *political science*?

* Plato suggests that you can achieve the same kind of professionalism in politics that you have in medicine. Politics would not just be a matter of *opinion*, but of *knowledge*. It is possible to turn politics into a noble profession.

Plato is arguing here that politicians *should* be like physicians, not that they *are*. The whole of Plato's response hinges upon the belief that there are eternal standards (the Forms). That political rule and, it follows, the practice of right conduct, of justice, can be based on knowledge, not just opinion, and that rulers, if they should possess this knowledge, would use it wisely and for the common good. When Plato makes reference to the science, or skill, of the doctor the word **_techne_** is used. In the same way that the doctor has the _techne_ to heal, the carpenter to make wood, the horse-trainer to train horses, and so on, the politician can have the _techne_ to rule.

Glaucon and the Myth of Gyges

The next character to take part in the discussion is Glaucon, who in history was one of Plato's brothers. Glaucon is also a Sophist, but of a lighter temperament than Thrasymachus. He has sympathy with the view presented by Socrates but is not entirely satisfied with it. Rather than attacking Socrates in the rather dogmatic and insulting manner of Thrasymachus, Glaucon prefers to play devil's advocate, to attempt to refine the arguments presented so far and put forward a series of propositions. Glaucon believes that what we need to do is to understand the _origins_ of justice before we can then determine its _nature_.

> ## KEYWORDS
>
> _Techne_, a Greek word which could best be translated as 'skill' or 'science'.
>
> **Social contract**, many philosophers have attempted to make links between the make-up of society and human nature and have suggested that humans form a 'social contract': that is they agree to form a society and live under certain rules.

Glaucon rejects the view of Polemarchus that our ideas of justice come from the gods, or from some eternal realm. He presents a **social contract**: when we trace the origins of Man, he formed societies and agreed to conform to certain moral standards as a form of protection. People followed justice not because it is an eternal truth, but because it is convenient to do so; it provides security and protection. People behave because they are afraid. If they go outside the law then they know they may get caught and punished. Justice, then, is a compromise between what is most desired (being unjust and avoiding punishment) and what is undesired (suffering injustice without any redress).

Glaucon is presenting a view of human nature not unlike that of Thrasymachus: it is human nature to be selfish, but right conduct is a product of a selfish act in the sense that there is an awareness that it is a convenient way of maintaining order in society. Although this might appear a selfless act, the individual would, if he could get away with it, be unjust!

Being good, Glaucon suggests, goes against the grain of human nature. To demonstrate this, Glaucon recounts the Myth of Gyges: One day an earthquake caused a huge chasm in the ground to appear where Gyges, a shepherd in the service of the king of Lydia, was tendering his flock. The shepherd descends into the chasm where he finds, amongst many other things, a corpse. From the finger of the corpse, he takes a ring and makes his way out. At a meeting of fellow shepherds, he was fiddling with the ring when his companions started to talk about him as if he wasn't there. Eventually, he realized that twisting the ring in a certain way caused him to be invisible. Realizing the power this gave him, Gyges used it to seduce the queen, murder the king, and seize the throne for himself.

Glaucon then asks Socrates to imagine that two such rings existed; one for the man who had spent his life being unjust, and one for the man who had spent his life being just. In this experiment, Glaucon wonders, would the just man really be able to resist the temptations that the ring gave him? Would not the fact that he could steal things from the market, murder people without being discovered, and generally be like a god make the just man behave just like the unjust man so that the two could not be distinguished from each other? The just man would soon learn that injustice is the happier option.

THE SOUL OF THE STATE

Plato now has to prove that justice is preferable; not because it leads to success and material benefits, but because it is a good *in itself*. In other words, the true nature of man, his very soul, is to be just. It is at this point that Plato launches into his description of the ideal state, of his 'republic'. For, he argues, **to understand the soul of the individual you have to understand the soul of the state that is the individual writ large**. As justice can be a characteristic of the individual and society, it will help, Socrates argues, to look first to the State – like placing a magnifying glass over justice to make it easier to identify – and then to find something similar in the individual.

Socrates does agree with Glaucon that there is a 'Gyges gene' in all of us, but there is also a tremendous capacity to be rational and good. The fact that individuals may behave like Gyges is not because individuals are naturally inclined to behave that way, but because society has *made* them that way.

What Plato aims to show is that for man to be true to himself, to be able to exercise his true *arete*, he must be allowed to do so through the encouragement of the State, his educator. What is at fault is Athenian society for producing people who selfishly pursue their own interests, whereas the 'natural state' would be one that would allow the individual to act according to his nature; self-discipline through the dominance of reason. Athens is a corrupt city and it must be purged through three waves of change that sweep away the old system.

❋ ❋ ❋ SUMMARY ❋ ❋ ❋

● Plato links his views on knowledge and the soul with his political and educational theories.

● Following on from Socrates' main concern, Plato addresses the question of the right way for a person to live.

● Plato considers differing views on the nature of justice and aims to demonstrate that it is better and natural to be a just person rather than an unjust person.

● To show that Man is naturally just, Plato believes it is important to outline the just State because the individual is effectively a microcosm of the State.

7 The Ideal State

Although many Athenians saw their city-state, their '*polis*', as the perfect ideal, emphasizing the city's cultural and military achievements, Socrates had taught Plato to be wary of a community that gives no place to those who have expertise in politics. Plato was only too aware of the darker side of Athens: its contempt and cruelty towards other states, its own arrogance, its serious political and military mistakes, and injustices towards its own citizens. For Plato, Athens could hardly be considered the Greek ideal. Yet, the fact that there might well be an ideal – Plato's 'City of the Forms' – encouraged Plato to study and teach political science. In the *Republic* especially, Plato constructs a detailed account of a new society; the ideal *polis*. To create this new society, three major changes have to take place. These are the three 'waves' that will wash away the old, corrupt society and replace it with the new:

1. A new ruling class of Guardians must be established who will be Philosopher-Kings.

2. These Guardians will consist of men and women.

3. The Guardian class will have no private property and will live communally.

These three measures were not only radical for their time, they can also be seen to be so in more recent times. Plato has still yet to define what he means by justice. He believes, however, that if we look at the principles that make up a just state we can then transfer these to the individual. Plato, through the character of Socrates, begins by considering the basic requirements to create a social structure.

THE 'CITY OF PIGS'

Socrates rejects Glaucon's social contract theory. Rather, men are not born self-sufficient and they cannot satisfy their needs alone. Socrates describes the formation of the State in the following stages:

* A state is when a group of people gather and settle in one place who have different various requirements.

* This gathering engages in mutual exchange, depending upon the needs of each individual.

* The most important of these needs is food, followed by shelter and clothing.

* In order to satisfy these demands, the individuals will take on various tasks; one will be a farmer, another a builder, a third a weaver, a fourth a shoemaker, and so on.

* In this state it is more logical and sensible that each person should do his specific task according to his abilities. The farmer should develop his farming abilities, providing food not only for himself, but also for the others in the community. Likewise, the shoemaker should concentrate on shoemaking for the whole community. This is better than the farmer only producing food for himself, then having to spend the rest of his time also making shoes for himself, building a house, etc.

* Socrates then goes on to explain this community in more detail. The need for craftsman, shepherds, tradesmen, a market-place and a currency, and shopkeepers.

* Finally, Socrates has presented a community that satisfies all the basic needs; consisting of a relatively small number where each has his allotted trade in life.

What is envisioned is a community of philosophic-minded people who have no interest in acquiring wealth and possessions, or in satisfying one pleasure after another. They would require only the essentials of life and live a love of Truth. The material world, for Plato, was a transient one, and so why would you want to load yourself up with material things that distract from the pursuit of the awareness of the Realm of the Forms?

Plato here presents a very idyllic, romantic vision of society. But Plato's brother, Glaucon, describes it as a 'city of pigs' because it does not satisfy the needs of the civilized man. Where are the comforts and luxuries? What Plato pictured was a state that satisfied the basic economic needs, without any mention of a political structure. In fact, Plato saw this basic *polis* as the ideal because people would live long due to a healthy diet and, most likely, there would be no need for a government – it would be effectively self-governing. Conflicts can be settled through rational arbitration, although it would be such a moral community anyway that there would not be much need for forceful policing. Also, as a philosopher, Plato would have felt that there would be no need for luxuries. Indeed, Socrates himself lived a very frugal life.

However, in order to determine how injustice occurs in society, Plato is prepared to paint a picture of society with the luxuries of life, obviously believing that it is these elements that disrupt the healthy and ideal *polis*.

THE CIVILIZED STATE
The civilized state would possess the following elements:

* The *polis* will no longer be a small community. It will be swollen in size because of the need for people catering for needs that are not basic. For example, artists, sculptors, embroiderers, painters, musicians, poets, dancers, and more servants.

* Inevitably, wealth will lead to greed, envy, jealousy and increased conflict. Many more doctors will be required because of greater ill-health due to over-indulgence in luxurious foods and stressful living.

❋ To feed these people, more land will be required which will mean infringing on the territory of other states. This will lead to war, and so soldiers will also be needed. Further, to maintain unity for this large and multifarious state, rulers will be needed. These soldiers and rulers make up what Plato calls the Guardians.

THE THREE CLASSES

Plato believed that injustice is caused by disharmony in society. If society functions so that the intellect rules and is not distracted by desire, then you have a healthy and just community. However, as Glaucon pointed out, this ideal is not a realistic one, for societies are much more complex than this and basic needs must include such things as theatre, music, art, and good food. Accepting this, Socrates wonders how justice can possibly be maintained in such a society. Here he presents the need for government and a strict division of society into three classes:

❋ **The Rulers**   The Rulers make up the upper echelon of the Guardians of the *polis*. They effectively govern the State.

❋ **The Auxiliaries**   These make up the lower echelon of the Guardians. These are the military. This fits in with Plato's belief that the best society should concentrate on specialization; each to his trade. Normally, all citizens of the *polis* were considered as potential soldiers should the need arise, but Plato saw the merits of having a section of society specifically trained in the art of fighting.

❋ **The Money-makers**   This, the economic class, consists of the farmers, artisans and traders. Basically, anyone who is not involved in governmental or military affairs.

For the rest of the *Republic*, Plato concentrates mostly on the education and character of the Guardians. As a single group they possess talents that lend them to a philosophic nature. However, the Rulers will be the ones that will engage in more advanced philosophical study and so will be separated from the Auxiliaries depending on their temperament.

The Rulers will have a more intellectual, rational and contemplative temperament, while the Auxiliaries will have a more spirited and fierce quality, but will be obedient to the Rulers.

The third class will continue to exercises their appetites as they see fit, and their function is to satisfy the economic needs of the State. The third class, incidentally, are not 'working class', as they are able to own property and make money. However, Plato points out that measures need to be taken to avoid excessive wealth or, for that matter, poverty.

The structure of this *polis* would, therefore, be made up like this:

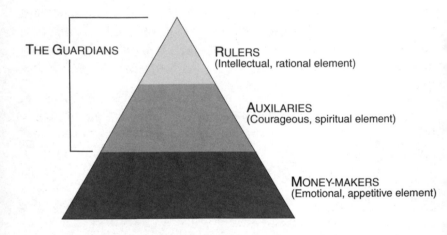

THE GUARDIANS

RULERS
(Intellectual, rational element)

AUXILARIES
(Courageous, spiritual element)

MONEY-MAKERS
(Emotional, appetitive element)

Really, there should be a fourth strata, that of the slaves. However, Plato assumed that any society would require slaves and they were not, in Plato's time, considered as possessing any rights. This, of course, strikes us as shocking today, but it must be remembered that Plato was writing at a time when any society of any degree of sophistication required a slave-class in order to function. The fact that Plato did not see this as in any way immoral may well be an argument for moral relativism! It does certainly show that Plato was a product of his time.

THE LIFESTYLE OF THE GUARDIANS

In order for this *polis* to function as a unity, Plato highlights the importance that the Guardians receive the right education and live a certain lifestyle, otherwise the state would be just as corrupt as any other. At first impression, this might well be the conclusion, as it appears that this caste-system would allow the Rulers and Auxiliaries to have immense power. Plato does not deny that they would possess the power, both in terms of political and military. However, remember that Plato believed that power could be wielded wisely and for the good of the community, *provided* those who have the power are brought up correctly.

Socrates says that the Guardians should possess the same qualities as a good watchdog, that of courage, strength and loyalty. The Guardians are to be gentle and protective towards their own, and also dangerous and fierce towards their enemies. Socrates also believed that as a dog loves those he knows, it therefore has a love of knowledge, and so has that essential quality; a philosophic nature!

Socrates argues that the Guardians must lead a lifestyle that will enable them to perform their duties whilst avoiding the temptations that power can offer and, as a result, doing damage to the community. Therefore, the Guardians must always act in the interests of the *polis* as a whole, and not for their own selfish concerns. How can this be achieved? The picture Plato paints of the Guardian's lifestyle is a radical, some might say communistic one, with very strict conditions (the Money-making class, of course, will not be governed by any of these rules):

* The Guardians are to have no personal wealth or own any property. As they will share things, there will be no dissension, envy or jealousy. They will not be concerned with the acquisition of wealth, and will not fight over who possesses what.

* They are to have no family ties and are to live communally. Plato saw the family, especially the complex kinship ties that existed in his

time, as a divisive force that encourages selfishness rather than a concern for the community as a whole.

✳ Men and women are to be seen as equals provided they share the same capabilities. This was certainly the most radical and, for many Greeks at the time, shocking proposal. However, Plato saw this purely from a practical perspective in that not using women is a waste of half the population of Athens. Women and men differ only in a bodily sense, not in qualities of the intellect or character.

✳ The children will also be brought up communally, bred and raised in common, with no specific mother or father. Adult Guardians will regard every child as their own, and the children will see every Guardian as their parent. This would result in an 'extended loyalty' as you will see all others as your family.

This lifestyle is actually modelled on a real society; the arch enemy of Athens, the *polis* of Sparta. To live a 'Spartan lifestyle' has now entered everyday language and is synonymous with austerity and discipline. The Spartans were single-mindedly devoted to the State and they lived a continuous military existence, living communally in barracks. However, despite certain qualities that Plato admired, he also found them to be deficient in a number of respects. For example, the Spartans had a system known as **helotry**. The helots were slaves who worked the Spartan land. These helots were treated far more severely than the slaves of Athens, being perceived as little more than animals and were even hunted and killed as part of military practice. Not surprisingly, helots frequently revolted against

> **KEYWORD**
>
> Helotry, a helot is a serf or a slave. In Sparta, people conquered by Spartans were used as their serfs.

their overlords, which meant that the Spartans had to be continually on their guard. Further, the Spartans were not renowned for their intellect, and their stupidity was mocked in Aristophanes's famous play *Lysistrata*. Certainly, the Spartans would not have Plato's requirement of a philosophic nature!

THE 'NOBLE LIE'

How will Plato maintain this strict division of the classes? Plato argues that his *polis* should introduce a 'magnificent myth' or 'fine fiction'. This myth will be taught to all three classes of the *polis* and will teach that all members of the city are brothers, born of Mother Earth, and forged within her womb. And so the very land they live on is their mother, and its entire people are brothers forged from the same soil. The Rulers have the metal of gold mixed in their composition, the Auxiliaries have silver, and the Money-makers iron and bronze. Knowing this, people will accept their place because it is their constitution, and it would be a terrible thing if someone of a lower metal such as iron or bronze ruled the State.

This myth has often been translated as the 'noble lie', although perhaps this helps feed criticisms that Plato is using propaganda. Indeed, Plato's most vehement critic, the philosopher Karl Popper (1902–94), believed the myth is typical of Plato's desire to create a totalitarian and propagandist state. It certainly smacks of inherent inequality and bears a strong resemblance to the Hindu beliefs that provide support for their caste system. However, Plato is recognizing the influence of myth upon society; certainly in his own day when the Athenians governed their lives and moral sense on the writing of poets and mythmakers.

Plato's class system was not entirely stringent. As all three classes are brothers, it is conceivable that someone from the Money-making class may be born with gold or silver in their composition, and likewise someone born in the Guardian class with bronze or iron. In such a case, this would be acknowledged and that person would shift classes. There is, therefore, a degree of social mobility and an acknowledgement of merit. Although Plato does not specifically refer to the education of the third class, it must be the case that they would get at least a rudimentary level of education to not only function as money-makers, but also to identify those who have philosophic natures. Likewise, if someone born amongst the Guardians proves not to have the intellect or courage required, they would enter the third class as a farmer or craftsman.

THE JUST STATE AND THE JUST INDIVIDUAL

Plato believes that this vision of the State will be a just one provided each section of society knows its place. The Money-makers will be able to pursue their appetites, but will be governed by the reason and spirit of the Guardians. Likewise, the Auxiliaries will have their spirit tempered by the reason of the Rulers. Here we have a perfect balance and, consequently, a healthy and civilized state. It is the social embodiment of justice. But would the Guardians be happy?

The picture portrayed of the life of the Guardians certainly does not seem a happy one, lacking luxuries or sensual pleasure. However, Plato believed they would be happy because the possession of knowledge is in itself a satisfying thing. Further, the Guardians would obtain satisfaction from the fact that they were benefiting the whole of society by their actions rather than simply satisfying their own desires.

THE HEALTHY SOUL

Having pictured the State as a whole, Plato can now compare this to the individual. The three classes function in the ideal *polis* in the same way as the three elements of the soul. The Rulers represent reason (the charioteer), the Auxiliaries spirit (the white horse), and the Money-makers are the appetites (the black horse). In the same way that the just and good city is kept in check by the rulers, the good and just soul needs to be controlled by the charioteer; not an easy task with two such diverse horses.

So, Plato's definition of justice is when the three elements of the soul, the psyche, *know their place*. The healthy soul, controlled by reason, is the just soul. In the same way justice in society is a harmonious relation between the classes, so justice in the individual is a harmonious relation between the different elements of the personality. Therefore, Plato is making a link between the just soul and the healthy soul. To be just is also to be physically and mentally stable and healthy.

Has Plato satisfactorily responded to the criticisms of the Thrasymachus and Glaucon?

✳ Firstly, Plato has to show that man is just by nature rather than convention. Glaucon argued that Man would naturally be unjust if he could get away with it. If it is the case that the soul's natural state is when the three elements function properly and are controlled by reason, then Plato could argue that Man, by nature, is just.

✳ Secondly, Plato has to show that it is to the individual's benefit to be just. Thrasymachus argued that it is better to be unjust rather than just. If Plato can argue that justice can indeed be equated with physical and mental health, then this would obviously be of benefit.

Much depends, therefore, on whether it is reasonable to link the just soul with the healthy soul. Plato's theory has similarities with the psychology of Sigmund Freud (1856–1939). Freud also divided the psyche into three elements: the ego, super-ego, and the id. The ego and the id corresponds closely to Plato's reason and desire, whilst the super-ego, the conscience, assists the ego (reason) by providing an emotional force to keep the id (desire) in check.

Plato believes that when desire, the appetites, are allowed to run free then we behave immorally. Therefore, when the three elements are not functioning properly we are mentally unstable and liable to commit immoral acts. There are, however, a number of problems with this:

✳ When someone acts immorally it seems far-fetched to say that they are mentally sick. There are many people who act unjustly yet seem to behave quite normally mentally. Even if it is the case that the mentally stable condition is where reason controls the appetites, it is debatable whether the rational part cannot be used to be unjust. For example, you can exercise your reason and self-discipline to rob a bank!

✳ What we consider to be mental illness seems conditioned by our environment. In today's society we would regard someone who thinks slavery is a good thing as 'sick', but this would not be the case in Plato's day.

* Freud believed that excessive repression of desire could itself be harmful and lead to mental illness. Plato's soul, like its analogy with the ideal state, is authoritarian and suggests that the appetites will be suppressed.

Like the psychiatrist who determines what is good for the psyche, the Rulers will determine what is good for the *polis*. This is based upon Plato's conviction that experts in political science can and should rule the State. Whether the day-to-day running of the State can really be considered a science is certainly a debatable point, although Plato argues that the Guardians will have the expertise required.

Plato places much emphasis on the need for authority, whether it be the rule by the Guardians in the State, or the rule by reason and spirit in the soul. For Plato, a 'democratic soul', like a democratic state, would result in a liberal attitude towards the appetites, which would be given too much freedom, which, in turn, would lead to immorality.

* * *SUMMARY* * *

- In presenting his ideal state, Plato believed that the desire for satisfying the appetites is what causes immorality.

- In order for justice to exist in a society, the appetites must be controlled in an authoritarian manner by the Guardians.

- In Plato's republic, there exists three classes: Rulers, Auxiliaries and the Money-makers.

- The Guardians, consisting of both men and women, will live communally.

- In the same way that a just society exists when the three elements of the society perform their function, the just individual exists when the three elements of the soul perform their function.

The Philosopher King 8

In the *Republic*, Plato presents a picture of three very different city-states (*polis*): the City of Athens; the City of the Forms; and the City of the Republic.

* The first, the **City of Athens**, Plato sees as corrupt. It is, remember, the city that killed Socrates. It is the city that does not allow the man of thought to practise his wares, but bows to the whims of the mob. Plato who, as a young man, had considered entering public life and becoming a politician himself became disillusioned with the state of Athenian society and the way politicians behaved.

* The second, the **City of the Forms**, is the ideal city; ideals that transcend earthy existence. Because it transcends earthly existence, the ideal city cannot be achieved on earth, but it remains an *ideal* that we should strive towards. In every way, it is perfect. The great Christian philosopher and theologian, St. Augustine, was heavily influenced by the writings of Plato and it was this idea of the City of the Forms that prompted him to write *The City of God*.

* The third, the **City of the Republic**, is the 'in-between' of the other two. As we move away from the City of Athens towards the City of the Forms, we can create a real and better society on earth. Plato was not just presenting a theoretical vision of society, for he believed it could actually be achieved, although – humans being the imperfect creatures they are – it might never be as perfect as the City of the Forms, it can get close to it.

THE CRITIQUE OF DEMOCRACY

For Plato, the problem with the democracy that existed in Athens was that there was no sense of individual responsibility. The city lacked a sense of direction, any real order or restraint upon the desires of the masses. The 'democratic man' had no desire for change in his life because he perceived himself to be free and happy, but lacked an adherence to civic duty. The *Republic* is not just a critique of democracy, but also a critique of liberalism, the kind of liberalism which allows people to pursue wealth and power but without any thought for the welfare of the State as a whole or, more importantly, with any concern for knowledge. What matters most in the Athenian state is whatever the opinion of the masses happens to be.

The Philosopher King

Having defined the philosopher as the lover of knowledge, and believing that there is such a thing as knowledge, Plato wanted to show that those who know how to rule the state should be the ones that do rule the State. Either kings should become philosophers, or philosophers should become kings. But Plato is confronted by a severe criticism from another character in the *Republic*, his other brother Adeimantus. Adeimantus is not quite as prepared as Glaucon to be so amenable. Although, Adeimantus argues, it may well be the case that those with knowledge of statesmanship should rule the State, it seems a ridiculous claim that this should be *philosophers*! Take a look around you! What a funny bunch philosophers are! Can they, argues Adeimantus, really make good rulers? If anything, they appear worthless and nothing but 'rogues'.

To the surprise of Adeimantus, Plato's character Socrates agrees with him. Yes, they are worthless and roguish individuals in Athenian society. However, Socrates intends to argue, this is the fault of *society*. It is society that needs to change if philosophers are to be true philosophers.

The Ship of State

To illustrate his critique of Athenian society, Socrates presents the image of the Ship of State. This analogy is not uncommon to us today, but it was first set forth by Plato.

* On this ship, this 'ship of democracy', the captain is bigger and stronger than any of the crew, but somewhat short-sighted and a little deaf. He is also no expert in seamanship!

* The crew of sailors constantly quarrel over who should be in control of the helm, although none of them has learnt navigation. In fact, the crew believe navigation is not something that can be taught at all.

* The crew beg and cajole the captain into allowing them to take control of steering the ship and, ultimately, those who are most successful at persuading the captain – whether through the art of oral persuasion or through more underhand means such as piling the captain with alcohol or opium – take control and turn the voyage into a 'drunken carousel'.

* The man at the helm then elects a navigator – anyone who helps in his quest to control the captain – regardless of whether or not that person actually has any navigation skills.

* The true navigator, the one who has studied the stars, winds and seasons of the year, is more than capable of steering the ship safely to its destination. However, the others see this genuine navigator as a star-gazer who spends his time in idle chatter and is useless to them.

How can we 'unpack' this parable?

* The ship itself represents the Democratic State. That is, Athenian society during Plato's time.

* The captain of the ship represents the citizens of the State; large and powerful, but rather deaf and short-sighted and lacking the skills of statesmanship. The captain can only understand the rhetoric of the crew, not the science of navigation.

* The crew are the politicians; each vying for power and attempting to persuade the citizens that they, the politicians, should represent

them. They will use any means, including the 'opium' of rhetoric. They are the Sophists, like Thrasymachus, who manipulate the mob but are not concerned with truth.

* The genuine navigator, of course, is the Philosopher King. The Greek poet and playwright Aristophanes in *Clouds* (a play Plato was familiar with) characterized Socrates as a 'star-gazer'.

This parable is not only an attack on democracy, but also the consequences of democracy; the emphasis on opinion rather than knowledge. Knowledge is not something that can be determined by the vote. For example, using the analogy of the physician once more, if you are sick you do not vote for the person to heal you who happens to be the most persuasive. Rather, you rely on the physician's knowledge and experience, as well as his concern for your best interests.

The Beast
Plato presents another parable to illustrate how the Sophists manipulate the masses. He asks us to imagine the keeper of a large and powerful animal. If the keeper is to control this animal he must learn its moods and needs, how it should be approached and handled, what makes it gentle or savage, the meaning of its language, what tones of voice soothe it and so on. Having studied all of this, the keeper will call this study 'science', reduce it to a system, and set up a school.

However, is this really what we can call knowledge? The keeper is not in the least concerned as to whether the desires and moods of the animal are good or bad, so long as they are satisfied. It is rather like having a pet monkey that likes eating bananas all day and never wants to sleep: you know you can control it by giving it bananas and letting it play all day, but you will end up with a fat and tired monkey! Therefore, it may be the most expedient thing to do, but it is not the right thing to do. Another illustration would be if you have young children. Do you give them sweets every time they cry merely to stop them from crying?

This is the meaning of the parable:

* The beast represents the people of the State. They are strong and powerful, but liable to be cajoled and persuaded so long as their basic needs are satisfied.

* The keeper represents the politicians, especially the Sophists, who are able to cater to the people's needs and call this 'science', when in fact they have no knowledge or concern for justice or right conduct.

THE TRUE PHILOSOPHER

Having presented these parables, Plato hoped to show why the philosopher is seen as worthless to society. In the Ship of State parable the philosopher is the star-gazing navigator, whilst in the Beast parable he would not be appreciated by the animal because he does not allow it to do as it wished. In Athenian society, nobody likes a know-all even if the expert is the only one who can prevent the ship from sinking in the middle of the ocean, or saves the beast from having a heart attack.

In the corrupt city that was Athens, the philosophers are perceived as useless rogues and here Socrates is making a strong case for the influence of society upon a person's character. Remember that for Plato – and for most Greeks – the individual was an integral part of society. If the community as a whole is corrupt then this is bound to affect the individual within that community.

Further, Plato argues, it is true of any growing thing that those of the finest nature suffer more from evils done to them than those of an average nature. The 'philosophic nature' is something inherent in certain individuals; a powerful force for good that, however, can be manipulated as a force for bad. A Jedi knight can become Obi-Wan Kenobi *or* Darth Vader! For example, a dog can be brought up to be useful to society, perhaps as a guide dog or a sniffer dog, or as a companion for the elderly. However, the same dog, if given a bad upbringing, could be vicious, attacking postmen and biting the hand that feeds it. The philosopher, ultimately, cannot be educated according to standards different from the community he is a part of. Should he ever recall his philosophical nature and wish to pursue philosophy once more, the peer pressure will be so great he will be compelled to put aside this yearning.

The 'common people' would not approve of true philosophy and will pressure those with the talents of a philosophic nature (courage, intellect, self-control, etc.) to use their skill for other goals, perhaps in business or entertainment. A modern-day analogy might be a talented poet who is compelled to write advertising slogans for a living because society has little patience or understanding of poetry. Plato argues that the reputation that philosophy has for intellectual vigour and wisdom will remain but, in the unscrupulous society, will attract rogues who, like the Ship of State analogy, declare themselves navigators but have little or no knowledge of navigation.

However, there will always be a few true philosophers; but society looks upon them like the useless star-gazers and they are forced to withdraw from society and only watch the corruption and decline of their society.

Therefore, **if the true philosopher is to be accepted by society as its ruler it is necessary for the whole of society to change**.

---

* * *SUMMARY* * *

- Plato considers three different types of city-states (*polis*): the City of the Forms, the City of the Republic, and the City of Athens.

- Plato argues that the best state, his 'republic', should be ruled by Philosopher Kings, but he must first address the criticism that philosophers would not make good rulers.

- The City of Athens represents the Democratic City. Plato criticizes democracy through the use of two parables: The Ship of State parable and The Beast parable. In these parables he shows why philosophers are considered useless to society.

- For the true philosopher to become ruler it is necessary, therefore, for the whole of society to change.

9 Education

One of the lasting legacies of Plato's philosophy is the value he placed upon education. Today, receiving a state education may be taken for granted by many people, but in Plato's time this was not seen as a duty of the State, and not necessarily a valuable thing to have. The *polis* of Sparta, which many Athenians envied because of its strict discipline and order, was also renowned for its stupidity. Although Sparta did have a state system of education, the content of what was taught and how it was taught was radically different from Plato's proposals. Even in Athens, it was only the aristocracy who received any kind of decent education, and this was left to the initiative of private individuals and organizations.

Plato was perhaps not so radical to suggest an equal education for all people. The education he describes is limited to the Guardian class only. His ideal *polis* would still have slavery, while the Money-making class would probably be limited in their education to what was needed to fulfil their tasks well. However, he did see the importance of a good education if you were to have a responsibility in running the affairs of the State, and that a good education was in the best interests for all in that State.

What is also important is *how* Plato thought education was to be taught. His teaching methods and his attitude towards the learning process says as much about his views on human psychology as it does about his philosophy. Socrates, of course, always believed that you cannot really teach anybody anything, only point them in the right direction, and this view is something that Plato was also a proponent of. You cannot force people to learn, to drill facts into them. Rather, you can only guide people in to how to think for themselves.

THE FOUR STAGES OF COGNITION

Plato's thoughts on the educative process are in line with his metaphysical beliefs; the belief that there is a Truth, a reality, a Realm of the Forms. Ultimately, therefore, the best education a person can get is an awareness of the Forms and, especially, the Form of the Good. The Analogy of the Cave is also an analogy for the educative process. As the released prisoner makes his way up towards the entrance and out into the daylight he is, painfully, undergoing a learning process. Another way to imagine it, is like steps up a ladder; you have to take one step at a time until you finally reach the top. These are the steps of **cognition** (knowing). There are four major steps:

Eikasia

The first stage is at the bottom of the ladder and it is the step at which, Plato thought, most of Athens was at. In the Cave Analogy, it is the prisoners tied up at the bottom of the cave. It is also the character of Polemarchus in the *Republic*, who readily accepts the traditional wisdom of his day and is uncritical in his thinking. In the metaphysical sense, it is an acceptance of the world of appearances, what Plato called *eikasia*; the world of images. For example, you may believe that you are a moral person simply because the gods command it.

KEYWORDS

Cognition, a philosophical term which refers to the action or faculty of knowing, to distinguish this from feeling and desire.

Eikasia, a Greek word that can be translated as 'appearance'.

Pistis, a Greek word that can be translated as 'common sense'.

Pistis

The second stage takes great effort to get to. You have to break away from the comfort and security, the belief that 'God is in heaven and all is well with the world.' This is when you begin to develop your critical thinking skills and begin to question the conventional views. In the *Republic*, the character of Glaucon might fit into this category. Plato called it *pistis* or 'common-sense belief'. That is, you have yet to be at the stage of knowledge, but your beliefs are correct ones, although you are not yet able to substantiate them. For example, you have come to your own conclusion that, say, killing is an immoral act, but you are not yet able to support and defend this view to any great extent.

Dianoia

The third stage is much higher up the ladder of cognition. Plato called this *dianoia* or 'thinking'. At this level you can engage in discursive thought. You not only believe something to be the case, you can defend it through discourse and logic. Although you do

KEYWORD

Dianoia, a Greek word that can be translated as 'thinking'.

not yet have perfect knowledge, you have arrived at abstract notions of reality. Through the study of science, mathematics and geometry, you have an awareness of abstract, universal concepts. As a rather crude example, you know that one dog and one cat equals two animals but, rather than concentrating on the differences in the nature of the animals (one is a cat and one is a dog), you are aware of the oneness and universality of the mathematics of one plus one equals two. Obviously, you would be aware of a lot more complex mathematics than this!

Episteme and noesis

The fourth and final stage Plato called *episteme* and *noesis*: 'knowledge' and 'intelligence' respectively. This is the true philosophic stage, away entirely from superficial appearance and partaking in the Realm of the Forms. Rather than having to engage in reasoning from premises to conclusion, you can grasp the conclusion itself by apprehension and perceive the whole structure of knowledge. This is the enlightenment stage, when the prisoner in the Cave Analogy can perceive the sun itself. In a more practical sense, it is when, through the conversational technique of dialectic, you are able to reach the true meaning of concepts such as justice.

KEYWORDS

Episteme, a Greek word that can be translated as 'knowledge'.

Noesis, a Greek word that can be translated as 'intelligence'.

Mousike, a Greek word that can be translated as 'music' although it has a much broader meaning in that it includes all the arts.

THE CURRICULUM

In order to progress up the ladder of cognition, the children of the Guardians in Plato's ideal *polis* follow a strict educational curriculum that consists of three elements:

* *Mousike* (the liberal arts)

* *Gymnastike* (physical education)

* Mathematics

For the children to be good Guardians, it is necessary for there to be a careful balance between these three elements.

Mousike

Although *mousike* might be translated as 'music' it had a much broader meaning in Plato's time than it does today. In effect, it covers all the liberal arts. Plato acknowledges the huge influence literature, theatre and music have in the formation of character and is well aware of its importance as an educational tool. In our modern society it is now acknowledged that young children in nurseries learn ideas and values through role play, music, stories and songs.

Equally, however, Plato believed the arts could have a powerful negative influence on character. In Athens, every child was brought up on a heavy diet of the great myth-makers such as Homer and Hesiod. Plato believed these were destructive rather than constructive; the only kind of character they form are those like Polemarchus; too accepting of the beliefs presented in these works. As a result, Plato presents a radical overhaul of the teaching of the liberal arts:

* Virtually the whole corpus of such works by Hesiod and Homer would be banned as these portray traditional heroes and gods as liars, deceivers, thieves, adulterers, and so on.

* Only stories that present gods and heroes as perfect, honest and truthful should be promoted. They must have a strong moral content that encourages virtuous conduct rather than praising immorality.

* In Plato's time, children learnt the myths by acting out the roles, what is called *mimesis* ('imitation'). Plato thought such acting would be bad for character as it could leave an indelible mark on young children

KEYWORD

Mimesis, a Greek word meaning 'imitation'.

embodying immoral characters. Therefore, acting would also be restricted to portraying only morally upright characters. Guardians must be single-minded and not have fragmented characters.

* For song and music, this too must be limited. Any form of music that encourages idleness, softness, indulgence or a lack of self-control would not be allowed. Music should be used only to express order, harmony and beauty.

Gymnastike

A balanced character also requires a physical education or '**gymnastike**'.

✱ Physical training will aim to produce good physical health as well as prepare for war.

✱ Diet will also be simple, with the avoidance of rich foods, so that health will be seen as preventative.

✱ The young Guardians will be taken to battlefields to watch warfare in practice to prepare them for adulthood.

Mathematics

When Plato talks of the ideal *polis* being ruled by Philosopher Kings, it is often misinterpreted as portraying philosophers as the 'head-in-the-clouds' type. However, Plato saw his philosopher as not only very practically minded, but also an expert in the sciences. Mathematics provides training in reasoning abilities and is to be encouraged from an early age.

✱ The very young children will not be compelled to study mathematics, but will learn the techniques through play.

✱ At a more mature age, the young Guardians will study arithmetic, geometry, astronomy and harmonics.

It is interesting that Plato's concern for the morality of our heroes has a modern ring to it, especially our concern with the influence of popular culture. However, his degree of censorship is extreme, and it is questionable whether the educational benefit of not having any awareness of immorality would be a good thing. Plato was the first systematic thinker to see education as important in the development of character, rather than specific education or skills. He makes no mention of attaining grades or passing exams, or being expert in specific subjects over others.

The American education system is run on Platonic lines, with an emphasis on acquiring moral and social values and relationships with others, while academic achievement is left till secondary education. Plato, too, is making special reference to young children, whose reasoning abilities are still limited. However, Plato can be criticized by enforcing too rigid a teaching of social values at an early age, not allowing the individual to be able to discriminate between good and bad. There is a large amount of conformity, no alternative schooling, and much censorship, yet Plato did believe that later in life they would become autonomous agents and intellectually adventurous.

THE FOUR IMPERFECT SOCIETIES

In presenting his ideal *polis*, Plato was concerned with creating a society that, by promoting physical and moral health, would result in a finely balanced and harmonic society. Remember that Plato linked the State and the individual closely; if you have a just and healthy state then this is mirrored in the just and healthy individual, and vice versa. There are, therefore, important parallels between the imperfect state and the various elements of the soul. Plato was only too aware of the inadequacies of, not only Athens, but also other societies, and he highlights these to demonstrate the importance of a good moral and physical education.

These four imperfect states are:

* The Timocracy

* The Oligarchy

* The Democracy

* The Tyranny

Timocracy

A **timocracy** is a state where rulers are based upon the degree of honour (the 'spirited' part) they possess. This state is really that of Sparta, and Plato presents it as an example of a defect in education of the ruling class. In Sparta, there was much greater emphasis on the physical rather than the mental, and this resulted in a warlike and aggressive manner that is divisive. As the timocrats grow old, they place more emphasis on wealth and property and the state turns into an oligarchy.

Oligarchy

An **oligarchy** is ruled by the wealthy. A love of money stems from the desire for things that money can buy, and so this state represents the appetitive element. In effect, Plato sees this as not a unified state at all, but two states; the state for the rich and the state for the poor. The

> ## KEYWORDS
>
> **Timocracy**, a state ruled by people because of the honour they possess rather than any particularly intellectual attributes.
>
> **Oligarchy**, the rule by the few, also known as a plutocracy. Rule is established depending upon how much wealth you possess.
>
> **Democracy**, a state ruled by the majority. However, in the case of Athens, only adult Greek males had the franchise.
>
> **Tyranny**, also known as despotism. The state ruled by force by one ruler.

result is excessive greed, and inevitable civil strife amongst the classes. In time, the poor overthrow the rich and democracy is formed.

Democracy

This, of course, is Athens, and much has already been said about Plato's critique of **democracy**. In a democracy the whole mob of appetites is satisfied. In terms of education, there is no credence given to those of intellect, rather for those who can persuade the masses. In time, a man will arise who can persuade the masses to follow him and a **tyranny** will result.

Tyranny

A tyrant, by Greek standards, was not necessarily a cruel ruler – rather, one who gains power illegitimately. As the democratic state sinks into anarchy, with varying forces vying for power, a leader will be chosen who will need to seize power by force in the name of restoring order. Having no legitimacy, the tyrant can rule only through the continuous use of force and the imposition of fear. In the elements of the soul, it is the dominance of the appetite for power.

THE ROOT OF ALL EVIL

At the root of all evil in society are the defects in education of the rulers. This is why it is not enough to provide an all-round education that the Auxiliaries, the soldiers, might receive, as this will result in an imbalance in the State resembling a timocracy. Rather, the best of the Guardians must pursue their studies further into the realm of abstract reasoning. This may take many years of both study and practical work before they can truly become Philosopher Kings.

✳ ✳ ✳ SUMMARY ✳ ✳ ✳

● Plato recognized the importance of state education for the welfare of society.

● He saw the educative process as an upward struggle towards the Realm of the Forms and the acquisition of knowledge.

● Plato detailed a strict educational curriculum that involved careful censorship.

● To highlight the importance of education for the State, Plato described four imperfect states.

Plato's Legacy

Plato died at the ripe old age of 81. He was buried in the grounds of the university that he founded, the Academy. His philosophy, however, continues to live and has proven to be a lasting influence on Western thought and thinkers. The most notable of these are Aristotle, Plotinus, Augustine, and Aquinas.

ARISTOTLE

Plato's most famous student was Aristotle (384–22 BC) who himself became a prominent philosopher. As a pupil of Plato's for some 20 years it is hardly surprising that his teacher made a lasting impression. Like Plato, Aristotle emphasized the importance of determining the right way to live and, also like Plato, he looked for guidance by examining human nature in order to show that living a just life is also a happy life. Aristotle also believed that man is a political animal; that politics and ethics are related and that the State has an important part to play in acting as an agent of virtue.

The School of Athens is a famous painting by the sixteenth-century Italian painter, Raphael (1483–1520). In this painting the two central characters are Plato and Aristotle. Plato, to the left, is clutching a copy of his most metaphysical of books, the *Timeaus*, and pointing up towards the heavens, whilst Aristotle motions downwards to the earth. Plato's emphasis on the heavenly, the transcendent, whereas Aristotle was concerned with what can be observed on earth.

Although Aristotle was a great admirer of Plato, there were a number of points on which he disagreed:

* Aristotle derived his knowledge from observation of the world. If something cannot be observed to be, then there is no reason to

believe it. In the case of the Forms, these cannot be seen, touched, tasted etc. Why, therefore, believe in them? What do they tell us about the way people *actually behave*?

* Ethical knowledge must be that which can guide our actions. How can the Forms, things that are eternal and unchanging, have bearing on the everyday world of changing situations and ethical dilemmas?

* Aristotle believed the soul to have two, not three, elements: A ruling element and a ruled element. The ruling element is rational, whereas the ruling element is irrational. Aristotle applied his theory of the soul to argue that these two elements, the ruled and the ruling, exist everywhere. Therefore, he argued, women cannot be rulers because their souls are dominated by the irrational ruling element. It is natural for women to be ruled by men. (He also argued that it is natural for there to be masters and slaves.)

* An extended family would result in the diffusion of duties and obligations. Fathers would not feel any sense of duty towards their sons. The family, therefore, is both natural and beneficial.

* Private property is important because it is not possible to be generous, to be able to give, unless you have private possession.

PLOTINUS

The Roman philosopher Plotinus (AD 205–70) was the founder of **Neoplatonism**. Plotinus emphasized Plato's more religious and metaphysical works in developing a form of mystical philosophy:

* The universe is the result of divine **emanation** from the supreme 'One'.

* The 'One', also known as the Good, is infinite and perfect.

* The 'One' also created the divine Intellect, which contains the Forms and provides order to the universe.

* From the Intellect comes the World Soul, which contains and animates the universe.

* The World Soul is the source for the souls of all living beings.

* There exists, therefore, levels, or gradations, of being: One – Intellect – World Soul – world of matter.

Man, though existing in the world of matter – the lowest gradation – also has the potential to access the higher realms. He can rise to the consciousness of the World Soul, the Intellect and finally to be united with the One when he has overcome bondage to the physical world. This can be achieved through moral and spiritual purification.

Neoplatonism, in a variety of forms, has had a huge sway on especially the mystical traditions. It was also a move away from the rational element of Greek philosophy to the more appealing and accessible emphasis on bodily practices for the achievement of enlightenment.

ST. AUGUSTINE

St. Augustine of Hippo (AD 354–430) was one of the eminent Doctors of the Church. This small group of 'Doctors' is given such a title in recognition of their contribution to Christian doctrine. Augustine was well aware of Plato's work and he is important because of his incorporation of Platonic metaphysics with Judaeo-Christian belief:

* The Forms could not exist separately from God as this would mean that God was not all-powerful. Rather, God created the universe *ex nihilo* ('out of nothing') according to ordering patterns established by the Forms existing in the mind of God. The Forms are the expression of God's Word, the *Logos*. The emphasis, therefore, is more on God than on the Forms.

❋ Augustine agreed that knowledge is innate, that it is contained within the God-given soul. However, Augustine believed there is another source of knowledge: Christian revelation as contained in the Bible.

❋ A direct relationship with God based upon love and faith was more important than the intellectual encounter with the Forms because the Forms themselves were dependent upon God for their existence.

ST. AQUINAS

Another great Doctor of the Church is the Italian philosopher and theologian St. Thomas Aquinas (1225–74). Aquinas blended Christian teachings with both Plato and Aristotle.

Aquinas accepted that there are Forms, but held that these could be approached through observation of the everyday world. The Forms are embedded *within* matter. Therefore, sense-experience is important in attaining knowledge, not just reason or faith. This is important because of its emphasis on reason and empirical observation, rather than the reliance on faith alone.

MODERN CONTRIBUTORS

Plato continues to inspire and cause controversy. His most severe opponent of recent years was the Austrian-born British philosopher Sir Karl Popper (1902–94). In his work *The Open Society and its Enemies* (1945) he criticized the political views of Plato because of its totalitarian implications. For Popper, the best kind of society is one that is open to changing circumstances, criticism, differing proposals, and problem-solving. This, Popper argues, is what democracy entails and he cites examples of democratic countries to demonstrate its effectiveness.

Although recognizing Plato's genius, he believed the mistake is in seeking definitions for terms such as justice, which, he believed, was futile and misguided. Popper argues it is wrong to be seeking a Utopia, when in actual fact we should be addressing the problems that exist in our society through immediate action.

However, others have been more positive towards Plato. One example is the novelist and philosopher Dame Iris Murdoch (1919–99) who incorporates much of Plato's philosophy within her novels. Another scholar and writer, C. S. Lewis (1898–1963), was often inspired by Plato. In his final Narnia book, *The Last Battle*, the land of Narnia comes to an end. The children of Narnia enter a new and more wonderful land. It is explained to the children that Narnia was not real, just *shadows* of the real world they now find themselves in.

There are many more influences, and far too many to recount. You could, for example, include the works of many Muslim philosophers who translated Plato's work into Arabic when Europe was still in the Dark Ages. Or you could look at examples of political states based on Platonic models, such as a number of medieval states in Europe, or the *kibbutzim* in Israel. Despite the controversial nature of much of his philosophy, the fact that Plato, after two-and-a-half thousand years, continues to excite interest is merit and applause in itself. Certainly, without Plato the world would have been a *very* different place.

✳ ✳ ✳ *SUMMARY* ✳ ✳ ✳

• Plato was a major influence on the other great Greek philosopher, Aristotle. However, Aristotle disagreed with Plato over a number of aspects of his philosophy.

• Plato's religious and metaphysical works developed into Neoplatonism, which is a philosophy that has contributed greatly to mystical traditions.

• Plato's thought has been integrated into Christian doctrine, especially through the teaching of St. Augustine and St. Aquinas.

• Plato's philosophy continues to influence, inspire and cause controversy to this day.

GLOSSARY

Aesthetics or the philosophy of Art – concerned with such questions as 'What is beauty?'

Analogy using an analogy is a way of explaining an often difficult concept by showing its similarity to more familiar things.

Arete a Greek word which can be translated as 'excellence' or 'quality'. Plato believed that all things have an 'arete'. For example, a pair of scissors' arete is to cut. Humans, too, have an arete. The difficulty is in determining what this is.

Aristocracy a form of government in which power rest with a small number of people; supposedly the 'best' to rule and concerned for the citizens as a whole.

Catharsis to relieve emotional or neurotic condition by means of relating a traumatic experience that has been suppressed.

Cognition a philosophical term which refers to the action or faculty of knowing, to distinguish this from feeling and desire.

Cosmology study of the universe as whole; its origins, make-up and so on.

Creation myth myths that relate how the world was originally formed. Common amongst most religions, for example Genesis in the Bible.

Democracy a state ruled by the majority. However, in the case of Athens, only adult Greek males had the franchise.

Dialectic a method of attempting to get to the nature of truth by questioning concepts. The Socratic Method is a form of dialectic.

Dianoia a Greek word that can be translated as 'thinking'.

Dikaisunē a Greek word which is often translated as 'justice'. However, it has a much wider meaning. It concerns the central issue of what is the right way to live your life and how you know that you are leading a good life.

Dualism a belief that there are two separate entities.

Eikasia a Greek word that can be translated as 'appearance'.

Emanation something that radiates from a person or thing. In Neoplatonism, the belief that the 'One' emanates its devine essence.

Empiricist empiricism is the belief that all our knowledge comes from our senses, from our experience of the world.

Episteme a Greek word that can be translated as 'knowledge'.

Epistemology also known as the Theory of Knowledge, and so concerned with where our knowledge comes from and whether it is 'true' or not.

Eros the god of love in Greek mythology.

Gymnastike a Greek word that can be translated as 'gymnastics' and includes all physical exercise.

Helotry a helot is a serf or a slave. In Sparta, people conquered by Spartans were used as their serfs.

Logos Greek noun which can be variously translated as 'word', 'reality', 'reason' or 'God'.

Materialist *see* Physicalist

Metaphysics concerned with the nature of ultimate 'reality'

Mimesis a Greek word meaning 'imitation'.

Moral philosophy also known as ethics. The study of issues such as if there is such a thing as good or bad and how we can determine this.

Moral relativism relativism means that all things relate to a particular time and place. Moral relativism, therefore, is the belief that morality has no universal and absolute standards, but is relative to a time, place or person.

Mousike a Greek word that can be translated as 'music' although it has a much broader meaning in that it includes all the arts.

Neoplatonism a 'new' Platonism that incorporates aspects of Plato's teachings into mystical religious beliefs. Founded by Plotinus in the third century AD.

Noesis a Greek word that can be translated as 'intelligence'.

Oligarchy the rule by the few, also known as plutocracy. Rule is established depending upon how much wealth you possess.

Philosophy broadly, the pursuit of knowledge, although – starting with Plato especially – it developed into a more rigorous and precise discipline.

Physicalist a person who believes that the world is made up of nothing but matter and that it is possible, therefore, to reduce all things to the basic fundamentals of matter.

Pistis a Greek word that can be translated as 'common sense'.

Polis a Greek word for 'city-state'.

Political philosophy The study of politcal systems and the asking of questions such as 'Why should we obey rulers?'

Psyche a Greek term that can be translated as 'soul' or 'life principle'.

Pythagoreans communities that followed the teachings of Pythagoras, which included a belief in the immortality of the soul, reincarnation and the importance of mathematics in determining reality.

Rationalist rationalism is the belief that we can use the power of reason alone to acquire knowledge.

Reincarnation the belief that, after the death of the body, the soul transfers to another body.

Social contract many philosophers have speculated upon the origins of human nature and have suggested that humans form a 'social contract':

that is they agree to form a society and live under certain rules.

Socratic Method a term used to describe Socrates' conversational technique of using dialectic.

Sophist a Sophist was, amongst other things, a relativist. Sophists were teachers who believed that there is no such thing as true knowledge. What is 'true' is what society believes or is persuaded to believe.

Technē a Greek word which could best be translated as 'skill' or 'science'.

The Forms every particular thing has a 'Form'. For example, the chair has the Form that is the perfect chair.

Theory of the Forms Plato's theory that the universe has an underlying order consisting of 'Forms' or 'Ideas' which could be ascertained through the power of human intellect.

Timocracy a state ruled by people because they possess a certain amount of honour that is considered more important than intellect.

Tyranny also known as despotism. The state ruled by force by one ruler.

FURTHER READING

Books written by Plato

If you have the money to spare you might want to invest in *Plato: The Complete Works*, edited by John M. Cooper (Hackett Publishing). This not only includes all of Plato's works, but some that are of disputed origin. Alternatively, the cheaper *The Portable Plato* edited by Scott Buchanan (Viking Portable Library) includes parts of Plato's major works.

I recommend as your best starting point a few of Plato's shorter works (for example, *The Last Days of Socrates* see below) before then tackling *The Republic* (ideally looking at more than one translation of this to appreciate the ambiguity of translating from ancient Greek).

Here are a few starting points:

The Last Days of Socrates, which contains Euthyphro, the Apology, Crito, and Phaedo, translated by Hugh Tredennick, Penguin.
The Republic, translated by Desmond Lee, Penguin.
The Republic, translated by F.M. Cornford, OUP.
Gorgias, translated by Walter Hamilton, Penguin.
Theaetetus, translated by M.J. Levett, Hackett Publishing Company.
The Symposium, translated by Walter Hamilton, Penguin.
Protagoras and Meno, translated by W.K.C. Guthrie, Penguin.

Books about Plato and his work

As little is known about Plato's life, much that is written inevitably concentrates on his work. The Melling and Hare are good as general introductions, whereas the Annas especially will help to guide you through the *Republic*.

Plato, R.M. Hare, OUP.
Understanding Plato, David Melling, OUP
An Introduction to Plato's Republic, Julia Annas, OUP.
Plato's Republic, R.C. Cross and A.D. Woozley, Macmillan

INDEX

FREUD – A BEGINNER'S GUIDE

Ruth Berry

Freud – A Beginner's Guide introduces you to the 'father of psychoanalysis' and his work. No need to wrestle with difficult concepts as key ideas are presented in a clear and jargon-free way.

Ruth Berry's informative text explores:

- Freud's background and the times he lived in
- the development of psychoanalysis
- the ideas surrounding Freud's work on the unconscious.

The facts … the concepts … the ideas …

WITTGENSTEIN – A BEGINNER'S GUIDE

Sean Sheehan

Wittgenstein – A Beginner's Guide introduces you to the life and work of this twentieth-century philosopher. Use this introductory guide to help you unravel his philosophy and explore his works.

Sean Sheehan's informative text explores:

- Wittgenstein's background and the times he lived in
- Wittgenstein's compelling personality and the course of his life
- the central ideas of Wittgenstein's work in simple terms
- Wittgenstein's continuing importance to philosophy and contemporary thought.

The facts … the concepts … the ideas …